on track ...

Joni Mitchell

every album, every song

Peter Kearns

sonicbondpublishing.com

Sonicbond Publishing Limited
www.sonicbondpublishing.co.uk
Email: info@sonicbondpublishing.co.uk

First Published in the United Kingdom 2021
First Published in the United States 2021

British Library Cataloguing in Publication Data:
A Catalogue record for this book is available from the British Library

ISBN 978-1-78952-081-1

Typeset in ITC Garamond & ITC Avant Garde
Printed and bound in England

Graphic design and typesetting: Full Moon Media

Acknowledgements

Thanks to Stephen Lambe.

This book is dedicated to the memory of musicians
Jaco Pastorius and Charles Mingus.

Would you like to write for Sonicbond Publishing?

We are mainly a music publisher, but we also occasionally publish in other genres including film and television. At Sonicbond Publishing we are always on the look-out for authors, particularly for our two main series, On Track and Decades.

Mixing fact with in depth analysis, the On Track series examines the entire recorded work of a particular musical artist or group. All genres are considered from easy listening and jazz to 60s soul to 90s pop, via rock and metal.

The Decades series singles out a particular decade in an artist or group's history and focuses on that decade in more detail than may be allowed in the On Track series.

While professional writing experience would, of course, be an advantage, the most important qualification is to have real enthusiasm and knowledge of your subject. First-time authors are welcomed, but the ability to write well in English is essential.

Sonicbond Publishing has distribution throughout Europe and North America, and all our books are also published in E-book form. Authors will be paid a royalty based on sales of their book. Further details about our books are available from www.sonicbondpublishing.com. To contact us, complete the contact form there or email info@sonicbondpublishing.co.uk *on track ...*

Joni Mitchell

Contents

Write In Your Own Blood

A print of a colourful Joni Mitchell painting once hung on jazz legend Miles Davis' bathroom wall. Mere weeks before his passing in 1991, he moved it to his bedside. In the weeks after, Joni produced a stirring Davis portrait in tribute, which, from an intuitive place of no-mind, rendered him in a kind of blue.

Rumours of a musical collaboration between the two had circulated for years. Uncertain whether Davis was keen on her music, Joni discovered only after his death that he preferred working on instrumentals. She would've gladly given him instrumental tracks to blow over. Davis' opinion of her was, in fact, reverential. All of her albums were to be found in his collection. The combined respect Joni garnered not only from Davis, but her regular collaborator, jazz saxophonist Wayne Shorter; the mighty composer Charles Mingus, and an ongoing list of jazz luminaries, was a virtually unequalled accomplishment for a recording artist operating ostensibly from a pop base outward.

To her, it was all music, and it was the quality of the music that mattered, not the arbitrary categorisation. Borderlines were non-existent. Music and painting were one. In interviews, she would often mix artistic metaphors, making it impossible to tell which medium she referred to. Throughout her recording career, she considered herself a painter first, but her mind was open to possibilities, her next move perpetually unpredictable.

Even at birth, all preparations were for a Robert John Anderson. The arrival of Roberta Joan on Sunday 7 November 1943 at Fort Macleod, Alberta Canada, changed everything. Her parents were Myrtle Anderson, a teacher, and William Anderson, an Air Force lieutenant and trumpet player. Music was established in the home early. At the age of seven, Joni wrote her first piece, a piano instrumental she called 'Robin Walk'. Piano lessons came later, but a stern tutor who would rap her over the knuckles for playing by ear put a stop to further composition for a number of years.

Contracting polio at the age of ten, Joni was cared for at home for a year before recovering. As a result, she was restricted to never lifting anything heavier than five pounds. The disease was also responsible for hand weakness, eventually requiring the need to adopt alternative guitar tunings.

Moving a few times, the family eventually settled 600 miles from Fort Macleod, in Saskatoon (The bridge city), Saskatchewan, the place Joni thereafter considered her home town. By the age of twelve she'd developed a passion for art and poetry. When seen one day by her English teacher Mr Kratzman, pinning a painting on a school wall, he stopped her, saying, 'If you can paint with a brush, you can paint with words'. But an epic poem she soon submitted – about a Mustang being chased and tamed – Kratzman flatly rejected, with the now-famous advice; 'Write in your own blood'.

At sixteen, Joni wrote 'The Fish Bowl', an anti-fame poem titled out of sympathy for the famous couple, Bobby Darin and Sandra Dee, whose marriage misadventures had become ubiquitous magazine fodder.

The fishbowl is a world reversed
Where fishermen with hooks that dangle from the bottom up
Reel down their catch on gilded bait without a fight
Pike, pickerel, bass, the common fish
Ogle through distorting glass
See only glitter, glamour, gaiety
Fog up the bowl with lusty breath
Lunge towards the bait and miss
And weep for fortune lost
Envy the goldfish?
Why?
His bubble break 'round the rim
While silly fishes faint for him and say
'Oh, look there, he winked his eye at me'

A life-defining event occurred after Joni drew a Christmas card for a boy at school. She was in turn rewarded with a copy of the Lambert, Hendricks & Ross album, *The Hottest New Group in Jazz*. The vocal group's adventurous take on the standards was to be a lifelong inspiration, Joni eventually claiming the album to be the only one on which she knew every song, including her own.

Just before a year's attendance at the Southern Alberta Institute of Technology at Calgary, she bought a baritone ukulele. Later, she taught herself guitar from a Pete Seeger instruction record. But not wanting to copy someone else's style, she quickly abandoned the disc. Her first real gigs came in the form of a few months work in late 1963, performing for free at the art school coffee house, The Depression. After friend and folk singer, Eric Anderson, demonstrated open-G tuning, Joni slowly developed her own individual tuning style, which in performance often required her to re-tune for every song.

The art education itself was a disappointment. The professors were interested only in the abstract, while Joni was seeking traditional knowledge. She has maintained that more tutelage around her preferred areas of interest might've resulted in a life 100% devoted to painting.

In August 1964, she took a three-day train journey to the Mariposa Folk Festival in Ontario, where she saw fellow Saskatchewan singer/songwriter, Buffy Sainte-Marie, perform. This journey inspired Joni's second song, 'Day After Day'. She'd forgotten one piece written six months earlier, so she came to refer to the new song as her first. Years later she would claim 'Urge For Going' to be, if not the first, then at least the first she took seriously. In order to cover the musician's union fees required to get gigs on the circuit, she took on a job in womenswear. Around this time she began writing songs at the rate of about four a week. In the fall, she spent several weeks gigging in the vibrant music hub of Yorkville, Toronto.

Fate stepped in in May 1965 when Joni met musician, Chuck Mitchell, at a shared gig at Toronto's Penny Farthing coffeehouse. One month later they were married in Chuck's parents' back yard in Rochester, Detroit, to the strains of a string quartet.

Basing themselves in Detroit in summer 1966, they lived in Chuck's fifth-floor apartment of the Verona building in Cass Corridor – a walk-up due to a busted elevator. They earned a living playing around the circuit as a duo; the show put together in a collage-like fashion. Chuck's repertoire had a heavy Brechtian bent in contrast to Joni's introspective songs of love-lost. Covers of folk artists like Gordon Lightfoot provided a middle ground. At Detroit's Chess Mate blues and folk club, they shared some gigs with folk singer, Tom Rush. He convinced them to move to New York, securing the duo a two-week engagement at Greenwich Village's Gaslight Cafe. Moving into a small apartment north of the village, they immersed themselves in the scene. But the pair disagreed on repertoire, and they separated within a year.

Joni had never thought combining some level of poetry with music was a possibility, considering the non-poetic lyrics of rock & roll songs. The exception was Chuck Berry, whose poetic imagery enlivened his songs. It wasn't until Joni heard Bob Dylan's 'Positively 4th Street' in late 1965 that a light bulb went off and she realised you could write about anything now. It was the song's anger that struck her – 'You've got a lotta nerve to say you are my friend' – the kind of emotion most pop lyrics till then had insulated against. From that point on, Joni's lyrics became more adventurous.

Travelling to the UK in August 1967, she conducted a short tour of clubs as a support act, commencing on Wednesday 23rd at London's Marquee, leading to a September appearance at The Speakeasy where she opened for The Incredible String Band. Returning to the USA, she undertook a week of dates at Florida's Gaslight Cafe at Coconut Grove, where on Friday 29 September she first encountered musician David Crosby. Freshly-flown from The Byrds, and in between serious projects, Crosby walked into the coffee house and was instantly floored by what he heard. Joni was singing many of the songs that would populate her first albums, including 'Both Sides, Now' which was already six months old. Crosby couldn't believe there was anybody around that was *that* good. Joni's act was by now finely-honed and she was ready for *some*thing.

That autumn she met her managers, Joel Dean and Elliot Roberts. After Reprise Records' A&R representative Andy Wickham saw Joni perform, Roberts negotiated a deal, which set Joni on the path to Los Angeles and cutting her first album, *Song to a Seagull*.

Upon arrival in Los Angeles in late 1967, Joni moved in with David Crosby, who would drive her around in his Mercedes, The Beatles' *Magical Mystery Tour* album as a soundtrack. At first put off by the dead pavements of a city that lived in automobiles, she was struck by how rural Laurel Canyon was despite its close proximity to the city. Its emancipation from the grid reminded her of Canadian lake neighbourhoods. The people were friendly, it was safe and no one locked their doors.

Many people took a shine to Joni. But it's beyond this book's scope to detail her romantic relationships any further than is necessary to outline a particular song. The focus is on the music. To reinforce her 1991 *Boston Globe* quote re music in general; 'Too much attention has been given to the artist, and not enough to the song'.

Further to that, seeming autobiographical traces throughout the lyrics are often erroneous. Joni has stated on many occasions her habit of taking details from her own and other people's lives, mixing up tenses and perspectives, in many cases authoring outright fiction where countless listeners and critics repeatedly professed revealing autobiography to dwell. Her songwriting was invariably approached as a form of theatre. In one interview, she confirmed this with the phrase that slammed the door on the subject; 'It is showbiz after all.'.

Some scrutiny of lyric is obviously unavoidable in an overview of this discography. But attempts to glean all-encompassing profundity have been largely passed over in favour of lean and tight quotes, the occasional one more closely examined. The lyrics are only half the story. In Joni's case, the harmonic and instrumental aspects of the work were equally as vital and worthy of discussion as the lyrics. Some tangled-up lyric theories as proffered by some critics and chroniclers of her key 40-year work period could be thought of as 'second-generation realities' – a term she coined when once referring to her early, sometimes oblique lyrics. As the years progressed, her preference was for the more direct shot of cinema. It became more a showing than a telling – more about the what than the who.

The search for the deeper meaning within this astonishing catalogue was once temporarily satiated when Joni threw us a bone with the admission that her favourite songwriting subject was 'the anatomy of the love crime'. The 'what' was really the thing from the beginning. The 'who' was occasionally Joni herself (but not as frequently as you might think), sometimes a friend, fictional character or all of the above. More often, the 'who' was the listener themselves. Thanks to Joni taking her old English teacher's advice to heart and bleeding in her songs, an open-minded listener was in the ideal position to experience some self-realisation, and benefit through Joni's graceful axioms.

Song to a Seagull (1968)

Personnel:
Vocals, Guitar, Piano, Banshee: Joni Mitchell
Banshee: Lee Keefer
Bass: Stephen Stills
Recorded in December 1967 and early 1968 at Sunset Sound Recorders, Hollywood, California.
Producer: David Crosby
Engineer: Art Cryst
Label: Reprise
US Release date: 23 March 1968. UK Release date: June 1968.
Chart placings: US: 189.

In Los Angeles in late 1967, David Crosby introduced Joni to the head of Warner-Reprise Records, Mo Ostin. A deal was struck with Crosby as producer. Crosby had warned Joni against using a name producer in the fear that they might decorate the songs with lavish string sections and who knows what manner of elaborate overdubbing. He'd inserted himself as watchdog in the first place to preserve the music's integrity.

The recording location was to be Sunset Sound Recorders on Sunset Boulevard. Waiting for a gap in the sessions for the final Buffalo Springfield album, *Last Time Around*, Joni was sidetracked to the newly-opened Studio 2. *Song to a Seagull* would be the first album recorded there.

Crosby planned on minimal instrumentation and took a hands-off approach to the recording. Not that there wasn't some trial and error. At first, Joni, in her words, went crazy, adding all sorts of vocal harmonies before they realised they were ruining it and pulled back. One successful technique was Crosby's suggestion that Joni sing into the grand piano with the sustain pedal down, causing the strings to naturally resonate with her voice. Frank Zappa had experimented with this several months earlier recording The Mothers of Invention album *We're Only In It for the Money* over at New York's Apostolic Studios. But most of Crosby's exercise was lost due to him later discovering an audio engineering fault. The tapes had an issue with crackling noise which the engineer Art Cryst had insisted was only in the speakers. Excessive tape hiss was also present. It was removed but unfortunately resulted in the trade-off of the album lacking clear highs.

Crosby, though successful as a member of The Byrds, was an unknown quantity as a producer. He and Joni were in the deep end, and engineer Cryst, though helpful, was ill and nursing a marriage breakup via drinking. Sadly he passed soon after completing the project.

Joni described the album as a conflict between the city and the seaside, dividing it into two parts and titling the sides accordingly with title track lyric lines; Side A: I Came to the City, and Side B: Out of the City and Down to the Seaside. The songs mostly had pop verse/chorus formats with the exception of the deeper side two material like 'The Dawntreader', 'Song to a Seagull' and 'Cactus Tree', which all bore the repeating single-section strophic folk format. Cover artwork came courtesy of Joni. The record was dedicated to her old English teacher, 'Mr Kratzman, who taught me to love words.'.

On cue with the album's American March 1968 release, Joni purchased the ranch house at 8217 Lookout Mountain Road in Laurel Canyon, which would become immortal two years later in the Graham Nash-penned 'Our House' from the Crosby, Stills, Nash & Young album, *Déjà Vu.* That single became an American top 40 and Canadian top 20 hit in 1970.

Four days before the *Song to a Seagull* release, and perhaps more auspicious in some ways, was the occasion of Joni's gig of Tuesday 19 March 1968 at the Le Hibou coffeehouse in Ottawa, Canada. The gig was business as usual with the exception that prominent rock guitarist, Jimi Hendrix, attended the late show after his Capitol Theatre concert. With Joni's permission, he set up a tape recorder. Sadly, both tape and recorder were stolen a few days later. A few months later, Joni would headline at the Capitol Theatre herself.

Side One: I Came to the City

'I Had a King' (Joni Mitchell)

Released as a single B-side, June 1968 (US and CA), 5 July 1968 (UK), b/w 'Night in the City'.

The willingness to be emotionally bare was evident from the outset. Joni here wrote candidly about her and Chuck Mitchell's marriage breakup in a pastoral folk style not unlike that of Joan Baez at the time. The acoustic guitar style was understated but forthright (and not merely because it was doubled), and deserving of as much attention as the perfectly-inflected singing.

> I can't go back there anymore
> You know my keys won't fit the door
> You know my thoughts don't fit the man
> They never can they never can

1960s references contemporised the lyric, preventing too much marination in fairy tale whimsy which was still practised by many a folk artist in 1968 (though Joni claimed not to be one), despite Bob Dylan's brutal 1965 collision with electricity changing the face of folk music going forward. Once asked if the song was autobiographical, Joni replied, 'Oh, sure. After I took half the furniture when I left, Chuck changed the lock on me.'.

'Michael from Mountains' (Joni Mitchell)

Michael was a friend of Joni's, an artist who she described in 1968 as a child-man. After some distance came between them, his influence appeared in both her music and drawings – a typical delayed reaction she admitted was not unusual in her work.

It will not be the purpose of this book to analyse every lyric or indulge in prosodic detail, but it's worth pointing out an early episode of this nature. Joni wrote songs well-imbued with the technical standards set down by the great musical composers such as Gilbert & Sullivan and Rodgers & Hammerstein, and the classic songwriters of the early 20th century like Irving Berlin and Cole Porter. In 'Michael from Mountains', the rhyme scheme from verse to verse was complex but locked in tight, with down/ground/found and an inner-line pattern of sweets/streets, tight/bright, and a triple rhyme of drain/arrange/change – a pattern followed to the letter in all verses. In such a straitjacket it wasn't surprising to find the weaker phrase 'Their mothers will scold' (Setting up the later cold/hold) sounding wedged-in after the fact, to make the triple rhyme work. This kind of fledgeling ambiguity would all but disappear from Joni's lyrics before long, replaced by other ambiguities at times perhaps, but those of an altogether more purposeful artistic nature.

Along with such techniques, the 'confessional' style as it came to be known, was already evident. The last verse was telling, as if her romantic inclinations interfered with her artistic intentions.

> There's sun in the painting that smiles on the wall
> You want to know all
> But his mountains called
> So you never do

The vocal melody on the chorus line 'Go where you will go to' wavered in pitch every time, as if she couldn't decide which note to choose, instead oscillating between the two. Either note would've worked. When it came to her music, Joni was not infallible at this point.

This song was a catalyst for moving to open tuning. Joni could never make a good F (or barre) chord position and avoided them at all costs, so she tuned the guitar to F for this song.

'Night in the City' (Joni Mitchell)

Released as a single A-side, June 1968 (US and CA), 5 July 1968 (UK), b/w 'I Had a King'.
Released as a single B-side, 1969 (FR), b/w 'Chelsea Morning'.

The first single release (featuring Stephen Stills on bass) was written as a tribute after a night out in Toronto's Yorkville; the city's then cultural music centre. Joni performed it on Christmas Eve 1967 on Toronto's *The Way It Is* CBC-TV show. But she quickly came to disregard the piece as insubstantial (Which she eventually would the first several albums), deeming the lyric non-reflective of the political reality of major cities with their hidden slums and police brutality. The desire to not gloss over such realities would increase in importance over time.

'Marcie' (Joni Mitchell)

Soon after Joni met up with her Canadian friend Marcie in London in the summer of 1967, they realised they'd recently lived two doors down from each other on Manhattan's West 16th St for two months without knowing it. The song was written in Marcie's London flat during an evening of Monopoly. Borrowing Marcie's name, Joni otherwise created a fictional character sketch set in New York but based on her experiences of London. The haunting descending chromatic chords perfectly reflected the lyric's loneliness, exposing the song as the first really substantial composition on a Joni Mitchell record. Its original title was 'Portrait in Red and Green'. Partial fiction or not, Joni was later to say that she herself was the girl in *all* of the *Song to a Seagull* songs.

'Nathan La Franeer' (Joni Mitchell)

This true story of a grumpy New York cab driver who took Joni to the airport, was written after she boarded the plane. It was her hope that the lyric might make a listener consider how they treat other people.

Personally, I never understood the logic when critics compared eccentric British recording artist Kate Bush to Joni Mitchell. But the vocal here, especially towards the end, certainly has an aspect that could've passed down to Bush's early baying intimate opera.

Side Two: Out of the City and Down to the Seaside

'Sisotowbell Lane' (Joni Mitchell)

The word 'Sisotowbell' was one of many acronyms Joni came up with working on a fictional mythology. Its character's names were derived from the acronyms of descriptive phrases – in this case 'Somehow in spite of trouble, ours will be everlasting love'. Some others were, Mosalm (Maybe our souls are little men) and Siquomb (She is queen undisputedly of mind beauty), the acronym used to name her publishing company.

'The Dawntreader' (Joni Mitchell)

Where the majority of Joni's lyrics at this time dealt with the trials and woes of the maintenance and/or loss of love, 'The Dawntreader' was a rare song of found love. It culminated in the third-verse peak of 'They'll say that you're crazy, And a dream of a baby, Like a promise to be free'. Such romantic fantasy (not to mention the rhythmic guitar style) harked forward to the *Hejira* track, 'Song for Sharon'. At this early stage, Joni was closer to that artistic point than we might think – ahead of herself as she would prove to be time and again. It was just a matter of the times and music in general, catching up with her.

'The Pirate of Penance' (Joni Mitchell)

Titled as a pun on the 1879 Gilbert & Sullivan comic opera, *The Pirates of Penzance*, 'The Pirate of Penance' similarly played out like a theatre piece. The lyric was a narration by the two characters Penance Crane and the Dancer, the former warning of the port's visiting pirate and his trail of broken promises. The piece broke up the album nicely, providing some levity, allowing for relief from the earnestness that weighed heavily in spots.

'Song to a Seagull' (Joni Mitchell)

The title track, with its themes of realisation and escape, was a lament to the big city which – for all its attractions and benefits – Joni felt was basically sullied by a falseness. The solution was to leave and become an anonymous hermit, living off the land. She would attempt something like it more than once, but it would increase in difficulty as her career progressed.

'Cactus Tree' (Joni Mitchell)

The fine album closer was inspired by seeing the Bob Dylan documentary, *Don't Look Back*. The song was written on Thursday 12 October 1967 in Philadelphia and performed that night at the Second Fret folk club. In 1975, Joni described the song as, 'A grocery list of men I've liked, or loved, or left behind.'. It expanded further to the idea of *any* girl who was busy being free and too predominantly driven by something else to concentrate on properly returning the feeling.

One of the men mentioned was real-life paratrooper, Killer Kyle. 'There's a man who sends her medals, he is bleeding from the war'. Joni had met him backstage after a show at Fort Bragg army camp, where he'd lectured her after exclaiming, 'You've got a lotta nerve, sister, standing up there and singing about love, because there ain't no love and I'm gonna tell you where love went!'. Kyle would resurface in 1988's 'The Beat of Black Wings' on *Chalk Mark in a Rain Storm*.

Clouds (1969)

Personnel:
Vocals, Guitar, Keyboards: Joni Mitchell
Bass, Guitar: Stephen Stills
Recorded in early 1969 at A&M Studios, Hollywood, California
Producer: Joni Mitchell and Paul A. Rothchild
Engineer: Henry Lewy
Label: Reprise
US Release date: 1 May 1969. UK Release date: October 1969.
Chart placings: US: 31, CA: 22

Arriving in England during the great flood of 1968, Joni was forced to recuperate from a dreadful cold. Invited by former Hollies and now Crosby, Stills & Nash member, Graham Nash, to attend the taping of The Beatles 'Hey Jude' promo film at Twickenham Film Studios on Wednesday 4 September, she had to decline.

Further promotion, including London gigs at The Revolution Club and the Festival of Contemporary Song, followed. In October, American folk singer, Judy Collins, released Joni's 'Both Sides, Now' as a single. It became an international top 20 hit, immensely boosting Joni's cause into the bargain.

Having become less prolific due to the sheer amount of time demands, Joni bought a piano once she was back home in Laurel Canyon, and began writing for the next album. The new lyrics added California experiences to the mix, though definite New York imagery remained. In New York there were so many potential stories in a single block that Joni could look at a stranger's face and immediately hear a song. In L.A., everyone was hidden away in automobiles, so the lyrics became more personal.

Commencing with the recording of *Clouds*, Joni forged a long-term working relationship with A&M Studios house engineer, Henry Lewy. Over a decade later, Lewy told US trade magazine *Music Connection*; 'When she first came into the studio she didn't know anything about the tools of the trade. In order to overdub vocals, she had to hold the guitar and pretend like she was playing.'.

The two clicked professionally, which was more than could be said for the assigned album producer Paul A. Rothchild, who Joni later accused of killing her spirit. Under him, getting through a performance was painful. 'I would be doing a take, sailing along, and all of a sudden, bang! – the voice of God would come over the microphone saying "You're off your mark" or "You're swaying to the right of the microphone" etc.'. After recording one song with Rothchild, he departed for two weeks due to prior obligations. Joni didn't want this producer changing what she was. Refusing to be babysat, she didn't need an ideas man suggesting the music wasn't up to scratch. She and Lewy then agreed to complete the album before Rothchild returned. With Lewy as head engineer and often acting as advisor, Joni self-produced from that point, right up until 1985's *Dog Eat Dog* album.

After encouragement from her now boyfriend, Graham Nash, Joni completed a castle and moat painting, adopting it for the album cover. The album art in general was overseen by Warner Brothers art director, Ed Thrasher, as had been the case with *Song to a Seagull*.

On Wednesday 30 April 1969, the day before *Clouds* was released, Joni and Bob Dylan officially met for their appearances on the inaugural episode of *The Johnny Cash Show*, to be filmed at the Ryman Auditorium in Nashville, Tennessee. They had dinner at Cash's Hendersonville home where, along with Graham Nash, they all sat for hours singing each other's songs. Another first occurred on Tuesday 20 May when Joni made her stage debut at Doug Weston's Troubadour in Los Angeles, where she played a six-night run.

Interest in Joni Mitchell was really heating up in 1969. A giant Hollywood movie company offered her a huge amount to write a movie about anything she pleased, and she turned down an offer of $1,500,000 to sell her publishing company, Siquomb. Topping everything off on Wednesday 11 March 1970, *Clouds* won the Grammy award for Best Folk Performance, the same honour awarded to Judy Collins' recording of Joni's 'Both Sides, Now' the year before.

Over time Joni would develop disregard for *Clouds* compared to its predecessor. She claimed to have adopted a level of vocal affectation recording *Clouds*, largely due to a close association with Crosby, Stills & Nash and their necessary adoption of a blending technique to help their voices meld. This exposure resulted in what she perceived as an overt American accent in her singing which died down by her third album. The sound was fine, but the unnecessary picking up of a habit displeased her. But the musical development since *Song to a Seagull* was plain to hear. Songs like 'Chelsea Morning', 'Roses Blue' and 'I Think I Understand' saw Joni stretch, as if eager to shed the folk appellation bestowed upon her to this point.

'Tin Angel' (Joni Mitchell)

The only track with a Paul A. Rothchild production credit, 'Tin Angel' was a solo acoustic guitar and vocal performance. Reading as half poem/half diary entry, the confessor listed the no-longer-required romantic items reverberating lost love, as an introduction to the revelation of newfound love in a Manhattan cafe.

> Dark with darker moods is he
> Not a golden prince who's come
> Through columbines and wizardry
> To talk of castles in the sun
> Still I'll take a chance and say
> I found someone to love today

The performance was a little stiff, probably thanks to Joni's irritation with producer Rothchild's habit of unnecessarily interrupting takes in progress. The guitar and voice – panned at eleven and one o'clock respectively – gave the odd perspective of Joni standing beside the instrument as opposed to wearing it. But the biggest sin here was the clunky tape edit at 1m:20s. It was likely less an oversight than mere technical happenstance plainly ignored, not by Joni I'd wager, though apparently out of her hands. It was unfortunate. No wonder she called the shots from here on out.

'Chelsea Morning' (Joni Mitchell)

Released as a single A-side, June 1969 (US and CA), b/w 'The Fiddle and the Drum'.
Released as a single A-side, 8 August 1969 (UK), b/w 'Both Sides, Now'.
Released as a single A-side, 1969 (FR), b/w 'Night in the City'.

The turning point that was 'Chelsea Morning' deserved to be heard as intended, as opposed to the plethora of cover versions that had crucified it since 1967. Versions by Dave Van Ronk and the Hudson Dusters, Fairport Convention, Jennifer Warnes and Judy Collins, were all examples of performer misplacement. None of them 'sang' quite the same as Joni's definition.

Wrangling with the song in the same session as first trying 'That Song About the Midway', at least nine takes were attempted before she was satisfied. Graham Nash watched on in support, at one point suggesting Joni give up for now, to which she responded, 'You just sit there and look groovy'. It was worth the effort. The final used take clearly emitted an energy and enthusiasm the opening track had lacked.

The song's inspiration also looked groovy – discarded stained glass windows found in a Philadelphia alleyway in 1967, which Joni set up as mobiles in her Chelsea apartment. Verse one was the sight track for the street sounds wafting up, the stained glass the prism for the morning sunlight, as was the actual window the prism for verse two's city view.

In a 1967 concert, Joni introduced 'Chelsea Morning' as being partly inspired by Frank Zappa's avant-garde group, The Mothers of Invention. She attended some of their notorious shows at Bleecker Street's Garrick Theater, though the group were not specifically referenced in the lyric. It was more the reflection of a happy period and not one she would later consider a particularly important writing period, despite the opinions of others. In 2002 she was to say that the real subject of 'Chelsea Morning' was innocence. Whatever the inspiration, the recording was a milestone, showing style development through the three-part layered vocals toward the end.

'I Don't Know Where I Stand' (Joni Mitchell)

You could easily construe this universal love song as part two of the love story begun in 'Tin Angel', but with the narrator in California on the phone to a love interest elsewhere. With a fuller arrangement, the song could've had hit potential. But one foot was mired in dreamy '60s folk molasses. The primary lyric offender, 'Crickets call, courting their ladies in star-dappled green', was likely an example of what caused Joni to later dismiss her early work as that of an ingénue. Logically, she could also have been referring to production flubs like the intro's guitar tuning issue, which spoiled an otherwise serenely beautiful performance.

'That Song About the Midway' (Joni Mitchell)

Attempted at the same session as 'Chelsea Morning', 'That Song About the Midway' demonstrated another elemental development in the work, anticipating the stark emotional intensity of the landmark 1971 album, *Blue*, but stopping short of its searing admissions. The fairground midway that set the scene, not to mention verse two's gambling/relationship pun, helped keep things light within what was an otherwise candid observation of Joni's relationship with David Crosby.

'Roses Blue' (Joni Mitchell)

An exotic deep-cut if there ever was one. In 1968 Los Angeles, you had your pick of gurus, and Rose, the subject of the overcast 'Roses Blue', chose at her peril. Joni herself was spiritual to an extent, but this lyric's warning exposed the danger of relying on mysticism and completely taking on a belief system to become a preacher in its service – something she was witnessing among her friends at a growing pace.

> I think of Rose
> My heart begins to tremble
> To see the place she's lately gotten to

There was a lot at stake and no punches were pulled here. Joni first referenced her friend by name, gradually distancing herself with the pronoun 'she', then 'her', leading to the ultimate sarcasm of 'To win the solitary truth you're after, You dare not ask *the priestess* how to think'. (Italics mine.) Clearly, there was no way Joni would ever fall for such a ruse.

> Friends who come to ask her for their future
> Friends who come to find they can't be friends

'The Gallery' (Joni Mitchell)

Any song was going to have trouble following 'Roses Blue', but it made sense to introduce lighter subject matter after it. By Joni standards 'The Gallery' was still mildly heavy, though nowhere near as dire, nor impressive, as the preceding landmark.

The reach of the song's thematic tentacles created interest. A strong connection was made to 'Roses Blue' with the subject of 'The Gallery' (a connoisseur of beauty, presumably Leonard Cohen) arriving back from the west claiming to be changed by religion. But the pointless pronunciation of the word cruel as 'cru-ell' harked forward to the 'Ladies of the Canyon' track 'For Free', which overused the technique. 'The Gallery' preordained this as lazy habit, despite its coming across as completely charming in 'For Free'. Joni was later to claim that she had no idea why she did it in that song which was otherwise masterful, but more on that later.

In her case, the occasional naive lyric line was more noticeable due to the otherwise virtually matchless surrounding prose. I point to 'I gave you all my pretty years, then we began to weather' as being a forward-thinking challenge indeed for the 25-year-old performer. On the positive side, the vocal performance was exceptional, reaching ever-higher harmonies, a skill Joni would come to experiment with more.

'I Think I Understand' (Joni Mitchell)

Joni continued to innovate her own aesthetic here. If you told me that Led Zeppelin took this song (and maybe 'Songs to Aging Children Come') as a cue to incorporating dark psychedelia into their initial blues bluster, I could believe it. Additionally, the composition was already three years old, making its prescient understanding of the human mind's whirring cogs even more impressive, certainly for a mere 23-year-old at the date of composition.

Some inspiration came from J. R. R. Tolkien's *Legendarium* trilogy with the borrowing of the word 'Wilderland', used here as a metaphor for fear as a location. This borrowing was perfectly acceptable considering Joni moved beyond the description to reveal astounding insight into the ability to accept, and co-exist with, common anxiety. For this, the song should be compulsory listening for all who seek assistance in coping with any form of dread or despair.

'Songs to Aging Children Come' (Joni Mitchell)

Requested to write a song to perform in a funeral scene of the 1969 United Artists movie *Alice's Restaurant*, Joni, short on time, offered up the pre-existing 'Songs to Aging Children Come' instead. The company agreed to take it but wanted a large percentage of the song publishing if they were to allow Joni to perform it in the movie. She vehemently declined. In the end, the song was performed by Tigger Outlaw in the funeral scene, an appearance often mistaken for that of Joni herself. But the differences were obvious. The movie version was completely bereft of impact, due partially to the dual harmony vocal being scaled back to one, and the performance was overly soft. Overall the song being likely misplaced in the movie.

'The Fiddle and the Drum' (Joni Mitchell)

Released as a single B-side, June 1969 (US and CA), b/w 'Chelsea Morning'.

This song's original title was 'Song for America' when written in late 1967. A protest on America's might, it was more in line with Joni's thinking later when it was chosen for inclusion on *Clouds*, though she felt these ideas were always expressed better by others.

In New York, she performed the a cappella piece note-perfect on the *Dick Cavett Show* of Monday 18th August 1969, the last day of the Woodstock festival. David Crosby, Stephen Stills and Jefferson Airplane also appeared. It was broadcast the following day. The song, striking in its recorded simplicity, was even more arresting uttered before the hushed tones of the studio audience – the vocal skill all that was required to deliver the message, aided by a simple key change up a tone halfway through.

'Both Sides, Now' (Joni Mitchell)

Released as a single B-side, 8 August 1969 (UK), b/w 'Chelsea Morning'.
Released on an EP, 1971 (UK), b/w 'Carey', 'Big Yellow Taxi' and 'Woodstock'.

Saul Bellow's 1959 novel *Henderson the Rain King* provided the initial spark of inspiration for the infamous 'Both Sides, Now'. One passage suggested that in an age when people can look up and down at clouds, they shouldn't be afraid to die. Joni took this to heart, or 'Got hung up on it' as she said later.

Begun on an aeroplane flight and completed on Thursday 9 March 1967 at the apartment of Joy Flevins and Larry Schriber at Center City, Philadelphia, Joni considered what she initially titled 'From Both Sides Now' to be a rock and roll song. This is believable if you consider the guitar's descending blues run at each verse's mid-point. She debuted the song live to air in an interview with Gene Shay the following Sunday 12 March on the *Folklore Program* on Philadelphia's WHAT-FM. Initially, she was fond enough of the song to perform it live twice, sometimes three times, a night.

Judy Collins cut the song for her 1967 album *Wildflowers*, that recording issued as a single a year later. Becoming a worldwide Top 20 hit, it won the 1969 Grammy Award for Best Folk Performance. Joni preferred singer Dave Van Ronk's more folky (but ultimately unsure) rendition. He even changed the title to 'Clouds', despite the theme prevailing only in verse one. Many covers have appeared over the years, including those by Bing Crosby and Frank Sinatra. The song provided much exposure for Joni, and indeed the definitive version was surely hers – perfectly in tune, heartfelt in a manner which Collins' candy-flossed hit platter was not, and resigned with a wisdom far beyond Joni's 23 years at the time of writing.

But she came to disregard the song, telling *People* magazine in 1985, 'It's young work. There are things I've written that are much more satisfying.'. Perhaps the idea of the song as young work was what drove folk singer, Pete Seeger, to write a not wholly complimentary fourth verse for his 1969 recording.

Daughter daughter, don't you know
You're not the first to feel just so
And let me say before I go

It's worth it anyway
Some day we may all be surprised
We'll wake and open up our eyes
And then we all will realize
The whole world feels this way

We've all been living upside down
And turned around with love unfound
Until we turn and face the sun
Yes all of us, everyone

Seeger's recording even had an unnecessary spoken introduction to this final verse, explaining (justifying) its existence. Though he claimed to be Joni's friend, a hint of sour grapes wafted. Both Mitchell and Bob Dylan had artistically eclipsed Seeger by 1969, and he might've been squinting a perceived oasis of irrelevancy on the horizon. His final word-landing of a non-traditional weak syllable on a strong beat (everyONE) would've certainly been cause for traditional songwriters of the ilk of Cole Porter or Irving Berlin to whack him across the knuckles. In light of Seeger's new competition, you'd think he might've nailed that last line. Whether he saw weakness in the song or not, it might've been best left alone, certainly considering how the song's strengths have prevailed across the decades, making it, if not Joni's greatest work, then definitely a yardstick of massive proportions for almost anyone else.

Ladies of the Canyon (1970)

Personnel:
Vocals, Guitar, Piano: Joni Mitchell
Cello: Teressa Adams
Percussion: Milt Holland
Baritone saxophone: Jim Horn
Clarinet, Flute: Paul Horn
Vocals: The Lookout Mountain United Downstairs Choir
Bop Vocal: 'The Saskatunes'
Recorded 1969-1970 at A&M Studios, Hollywood, California.
Producer: Joni Mitchell
Engineer: Henry Lewy
Arranger: Don Bagley
Label: Reprise
US Release date: April 1970. UK Release date: May 1970.
Chart placings: US: 27, UK: 8, CA: 16, AU: 32

At a Reprise Records reception held in London in January 1970, Joni announced she would be postponing all bookings indefinitely, including an appearance at Carnegie Hall. She claimed to need a break badly and felt her writing was suffering due to constant time demands. Save for her sole UK concert at London's Royal Festival Hall on Saturday 17 January, she would not officially perform live again until appearing at Toronto's Mariposa Folk Festival on 28 July 1970.

Now that she was writing on piano, the songs themselves were also changing. The new material was written at home in Laurel Canyon, as was Graham Nash's song 'Our House' which would become a hit for Crosby, Stills, Nash & Young later that year. That lyric basically played out like a diary page from the life of Mitchell and Nash. After the pair had breakfast one morning at Art's Deli in the San Fernando Valley, Joni bought a vase at an antique store. Returning home to Lookout Mountain Road, Graham lit the fire while Joni placed some flowers in the new vase. He then wrote the song at the piano, uninterrupted by Joni or their out-of-order antique grandfather clock that neither ticked nor chimed.

While 'Our House' might've been as universal and accessible as could be, Joni's songs were becoming a little more experimental and contemporary. The new recordings shed the folk uniformity of songs like 'Michael from Mountains' and 'Songs to Aging Children Come', absolutely for the better.

In hindsight, *Ladies of the Canyon* can be considered a transitional album with songs like 'Morning Morgantown',' The Priest' and 'The Circle Game' more representing the earlier period, and 'For Free', 'The Arrangement' and 'Big Yellow Taxi' demonstrating development.

In early spring, Joni took a break, travelling through Greece, Spain, France, and from Jamaica to Panama. During this period, Crosby, Stills, Nash & Young released their *Déjà Vu* album featuring 'Our House' and their take on Joni's song, 'Woodstock'. She also recorded the song for *Ladies of the Canyon*, released a month later. Her album cover illustration was the simplest so far, consisting of a line profile and a Laurel Canyon water-colour.

In general, reviews were positive and glowing, if at times inaccurate. *Rolling Stone*'s Gary Von Tersch somehow heard 'Woodstock''s sole instrument, the Wurlitzer electric piano, as 'A heavily-amped electric guitar'. Infamous *Village Voice* critic, Robert Christgau, found Joni's voice 'weak', and her wordplay 'inconsistent' and 'laughably high school', conveniently leaving little room for explanation in his virtual haiku-length review. He did, however, find the album contained 'richer, more sophisticated songs', within which phrase he was correct.

'Morning Morgantown' (Joni Mitchell)

Comparing early bootleg recordings of this apparent paean to Morgantown, West Virginia, with their *Ladies of the Canyon* counterpart, is a revelation. Joni's early vocal performances weighed some songs down with not only a Judy-Collins-like affectation but an upper-crust roundness to the vowel sounds, giving the songs a posture that sometimes clouded subject matter. Thankfully, that habit had all but disappeared by this point, now giving 'Morning Morgantown' an appropriately light and carefree quality, aided by the choruses' high piano arpeggios and subtle woodblock percussion.

'For Free' (Joni Mitchell)

We're really in album territory now – Kick off with a forthright accessible vehicle and complete the one-two punch with an undeniable artistic statement in danger of dwarfing whatever follows.

Stories conflict over the true inspiration for this tale of observing a busking clarinettist. In 1973 the UK's *New Musical Express* claimed the song referred to Canterbury scene saxophonist, Lol Coxhill. They went as far as to suggest the observed performance took place on London's Piccadilly Circus and was of the American traditional 'St. James Infirmary Blues'. They even boldly stated that the opening melody of 'For Free' was identical to that of the traditional. Listening today, at best the melody can be considered little more than a variation on the blues standard, though a similarity is evident.

A clue existed to the truth of all this in the lyric all along:

But the one-man-band
By the quick lunch stand
He was playing real good for free

The clue in the second line was ambiguous due to a lack of appropriate capital letters in the album sleeve's printed lyrics. The line actually referred to the Quick Lunch chain that flourished in Manhattan from the 1890s. Further to this, *NME* had in fact already quoted Joni as saying the song spoke of a street musician she saw on the corner of 6th and 8th in Manhattan. But this didn't stop the magazine throwing Lol Coxhill under the bus in 1973 by exposing his apparent quote; 'If she dug me so much, why didn't she use me on the session?'

Joni wanted to meet the anonymous New York clarinettist but neither her nor her friends on the lookout ever saw him again. But he was great song fodder, and the subject was deftly handled, passed through a musical filter of grounded sentiment kept in check by a closing flurry of jazz improvisation – a technique always so capable of maintaining a low emotional temperature. It was the first of its kind to appear on a Joni recording.

The return of the 'cru-ell' word over-enunciation previously used in 'The Gallery', helped to further curb the potential for heading into out-'n'-out tear-jerker territory, mainly by rhyming it with 'jew-ells' and 'schoo-ells'. Joni claimed to have no explanation for her use of the technique and later came to regret its inclusion. But the song had clearly flowed in the writing, and the technique bolstered the sincerity, helping keep any accusation of pretension at bay despite the newfound jazz leanings in a heretofore folk setting. Indeed the jazz voice would eventually become a more-or-less permanent fixture in Joni's work.

Stylistically, 'For Free' had a foot in the classical realm too, the inclusion of cello subtly flirting with a kind of third-stream blend of jazz and classical instrumentation. It was a mere touch though, the cello and clarinet barely crossing each other at all. The cello was even given its own goosebump pizzicato flourish at 3m:27s – a sonic detail reflecting the then ever-growing importance and prevalence of the album as art form.

In spite of Joni's later opinion of the jew-ell/schoo-ell vocalising, she retained enough affection for 'For Free' to add a further stanza for its performances on her 1983 *Refugee* world tour.

Playing like a fallen angel
Playing like a rising star
Playing for a hat full of nothing
To the honking of the cars

'Conversation' (Joni Mitchell)

Released as a single B-side, 1970 (VE), b/w 'Big Yellow Taxi'.

'Conversation' dates from at least 1967. The album version flaunted a lean and tight lyric expounding the woes of a love triangle – an entire verse omitted for the recording. Those fourteen lines were more ambiguous and abstract, not fitting the lyric's ultimate clarity – more validation of the argument for letting a song mature, so it finds itself. Joni was a natural at knowing when this was necessary.

She also had a knack for matching lyric content with vocal styling to create a third level of information for the listener open to discovering it. In this case, the often highly-strung soprano wail betrayed her usual coolness, but maybe that was the point. The occasional addition of lyric autobiography notwithstanding, there was no reason why every song need appear to be sung by the same character. Here we had a smart individual plainly laying her love-triangle problem bare, well aware of the pitfalls and consequences, even resigned to failure. But the vocal tone told a different story, exposing the anxiety, restlessness and torment immediately beneath the thin skin.

The acoustic guitar rhythm carrying it all foreshadowed that which characterised the album's hit single 'Big Yellow Taxi', though here with more subtle percussion accompaniment.

'Ladies of the Canyon' (Joni Mitchell)

As an album, *Ladies of the Canyon* suffered at the hands of its title track, which came across as something Joni could've written in her sleep. It had the air of a first draft, waiting for lines like, 'And filigree on leaf and vine/Vine and leaf are filigree' to undergo repair. Instead, each verse mirrored them – 'All are fat and none are thin/None are thin and all are fat', 'At bevelled mirrors in empty halls/Empty halls and bevelled mirrors' and 'And she gathers flowers for her home/For her home she gathers flowers'.

Being a snapshot of Joni's friends Estrella Berosini, Annie Burden and Trina Robbins, you get the feeling the song was originally considered as little more than a gesture, the thought of it being elevated to album title track status the furthest thing from anyone's mind. Once that idea came on the radar, surely a re-evaluation of the repeating high clashing verse vocal melody note that degrades the lines 'And her coat's a second-hand one' and 'She may make some brownies today', would've been worth considering. Not to mention the clunky chord-change that sticks its head up in those spots. In its defence, it at least doesn't modulate out of key.

Definite objectivity was lost in the importance and prime position allocated to this piece. By 1970, in the midst of an era when songwriters really had to be on their game to even compete, spotting writing misdeeds was where a savvy outside producer could really come in handy for an artist too close to their material. Engineer Henry Lewy would certainly have clocked these kinds of details. He might've seconded as a good buffer, but it's unlikely he ever got the final call on any musical thing.

'Willy' (Joni Mitchell)

Known to refer to Graham Nash, these two brief and affecting verses more generally address, on the one hand, the bufferless borderline that can exist between the exit of heartbreak and the re-entry of cupid, and on the other, the associated frustrations. The song harks forward to the blood haemorrhaged over the artistically triumphant following album *Blue*. But 'Willy' can be considered a mere bloodlet in comparison if indeed a slightly painful one.

You can imagine being completely convinced if Joni spoke the below lines to you. Therein lies the song's genius, in using the painfully personal first verse as an opportunity to teach the listener a lesson in the second, whether she's addressing Willy or not.

But you know it's hard to tell when you're in the spell
If it's wrong or if it's real
But you're bound to lose
If you let the blues get you scared to feel

'The Arrangement' (Joni Mitchell)

It's believed that this initial inspiration came via a request for Joni to collaborate with composer, David Amram, on a song for the 1969 movie of Elia Kazan's bestselling 1967 novel, *The Arrangement.* That arrangement never panned out, but Joni theoretically borrowed the story's theme of a love triangle for her namesake song written later. That idea fit snugly in the context of the album alongside 'Conversation', not that the triangle idea was obvious from reading 'The Arrangement''s lyric.

In hindsight, the slightly dissonant jazz piano voicings and lack of introduction tempo were an astonishing prismatic view into a future Joni yet to fully emerge. Even lines like 'Swimming pool in the back yard' and 'The wife she keeps the keys' predicted the thematic capitalist flourishes of 1975's *The Hissing of Summer Lawns* – an accomplished record indeed that would be perceived by some as difficult. But there were still artistic hurdles left to leap before quite reaching even the relatively accessible conceptual left-turn launching pad of 1974's *Court and Spark*. Up to that point though, Joni viewed 'The Arrangement' as one of the most sophisticated pieces she'd yet committed to tape, and it was certainly true for *Ladies of the Canyon*.

'Rainy Night House' (Joni Mitchell)

Originally purported to be about influential American disc jockey, B. Mitchel Reed; The fastest tongue in the west, Joni later confirmed the subject to be a rock musician 'Enshrined on the FM airwaves'. He remained nameless due to her wish to not limit people bringing their own experience or interpretation to the lyrics, though it was believed by some to refer to Leonard Cohen.

Like 'For Free', the track was piano-based but with more consistent cello lines and less transparency than that earlier benchmark. The multi-tracked vocals after the line 'I sing soprano in the upstairs choir' acted as another forerunner, this time to the thickly-laid chorales of 1975's 'Shadows and Light'.

'The Priest' (Joni Mitchell)

One of the most enigmatic compositions in the entire discography, 'The Priest' sat as stylistic filler among this forward-thinking collection. It could be taken literally as the meeting of a priest, as more symbolic of a romance, or even a combination of the two. Sounding as if culled from *Song to a Seagull* outtakes, it was for the hardcore audience and not an ideal introductory piece. But it did at least provide contrast and gave any newcomers insight into another dimension of Joni's work. More misplaced than unworthy, it contained another of the many killer couplets that would increasingly populate her lyrics.

Behind the lash and the circles blue
He looked as only a priest can, through

'Blue Boy' (Joni Mitchell)

If 'Willy' was part one, 'Blue Boy' could plausibly be part two. The earlier song was up close and in the situation, the piano more urgent. Whereas here, a similar situation was viewed retrospectively at the distance of the third person, astride more controlled piano-playing. The two songs could've swapped album positions, with 'Willy' being the lyrical stepping stone to the bravery of the coming *Blue*.

'Big Yellow Taxi' (Joni Mitchell)

Released as a single A-side, April 1970 (US), 22 May 1970 (UK), July 1970 (AU and NZ), b/w 'Woodstock'. US: 67. UK: 11. CA: 14. AU: 6. NL: 19.
Released as a single A-side, 1970 (VE), b/w 'Conversation'.
Released as a single B-side, October 1970 (JP), b/w 'Woodstock'.
Released on an EP, 1971 (UK), b/w 'Carey', 'Both Sides, Now' and 'Woodstock'.
Released as a four-song EP titled 4, 1971 (AU), b/w 'The Circle Game', 'Carey' and 'Woodstock'.
Released as a single A-side, 1975 (FR), b/w 'Woodstock'.

A visit to Hawaii in November 1969 inspired what became, if not Joni's highest-charting single, then definitely her most enduring. Hitting her high-rise hotel room late at night, it wasn't until pulling back the curtains the following morning that she saw the awe-inspiring Pacific Ocean in the distance and the ugly concrete hotel car park below. She wrote the song there and then, soon recording it back in Hollywood as a late rock and roll parody, which added an extra dimension to the line 'You don't know what you've got till it's gone'.

The lyric's pink hotel was likely a reference to Honolulu's Royal Hawaiian, and the 'tree museum' certainly referred to the Foster Botanical Garden where the 'dollar and a half' has since inflated to $5 'just to see 'em', or $25 for a family pass.

Fine Arts Films created an animation to accompany the recording which was broadcast on the second episode of *The Sonny & Cher Comedy Hour* on Sunday 8 August 1971. Though the film was an award winner in its day, in hindsight the imagery was overly literal, reflecting every single passing lyric line with little added imagination or enhancement.

The song itself fared better. As a direct result of its message, there were even cases of cities tearing up parking lots to create parks in their place. Over time, the jovial-sounding song came to be used in primary schools to help inform children on the subject of ecology. In that situation I can imagine the more personal third verse, with its reference to a relationship break-up, being omitted.

This was not Joni's most successful US single though. Some later '70s singles – most notably 'Help Me' – charted much higher. Even 1975's 'In France They Kiss On Main Street' reached a notch higher in the US. But 'Big Yellow Taxi' was effectively Joni's sole chart single in the UK until 1994's 'How Do You Stop' scraped the top 100 there. Ultimately, the Australian chart peak of number six was 'Big yellow Taxi's' highest placement.

Joni re-recorded the song in an even more spontaneous-sounding version for her final album *Shine* in 2007.

'Woodstock' (Joni Mitchell)

Released as a single B-side, April 1970 (US), 22 May 1970 (UK), July 1970 (AU and NZ), b/w 'Big Yellow Taxi'.
Released as a single A-side, October 1970 (JP), b/w 'Big Yellow Taxi'.
Released as a single B-side, 1971 (JP), b/w 'The Circle Game'.
Released as an EP, 1971 (UK), b/w 'Carey', 'Both Sides, Now' and 'Big Yellow Taxi'.
Released on a four-song EP titled 4, 1971 (AU), b/w 'Big Yellow Taxi', 'The Circle Game' and 'Carey'.
Released as a single B-side, 1975 (FR), b/w 'Big Yellow Taxi'.

After appearing with Crosby, Stills, Nash & Young at their debut concert at Chicago's Auditorium Theatre on Saturday 16 August 1969, they and Joni made it to the airport accompanied by David Geffen and Joni's manager, Elliott Gould. The two acts were to fly out for their Woodstock Festival appearances. At the last minute, it was decided against fulfilling Joni's slated Sunday night slot, as there were concerns for practically removing her in time for a scheduled appearance in New York on *The Dick Cavett Show* the following Monday. With the festival already well underway, traffic around it was reported at times to be in lines up to nine miles long. In 1988, Joni appropriately quipped to *Q* magazine, 'If it happened now I think I would've given them a good argument because it kind of broke my heart. But I was the girl in the family. "Daddy" said I couldn't go.'.

Forced to wait it out in a New York hotel, Joni watched the festival on television. She found it to be a revelation that so many could peacefully assemble, share their food and even have babies in the mud. To her, it was all symbolic of an idealism. After hearing Graham Nash's account of the occasion, she wrote the song which was not only concerned with the festival's spirit but also the political climate of the times. In 1991 she claimed the phrase 'We've got to get ourselves back to the garden' referred to the breakdown of communism being no victory.

The song was so personal to Joni that the first few times she performed it live, she had to stop once she started as she found it so moving. But a few years later, she was distanced enough from the song to refer to it as a mere news report.

In the recording, the track utilized a sole Wurlitzer electric piano. The instrument, already around for a decade, had yet to become a recognizable signature pop sound, despite its use in Ray Charles' 'What'd I Say?' and Marvin Gaye's 'I Heard it Through the Grapevine'. Being given centre-stage in 'Woodstock' likely gave the piano the boost it needed, then becoming ubiquitous and eventually heard on records by everyone from The Carpenters to Steely Dan, and most famously, Supertramp's 1979 hit, 'Logical Song'.

Logic itself played less of a part in 'Woodstock''s composition as it might've in other *Ladies of the Canyon* selections. The story of meeting a child of God on the road to the festival seemed more spontaneously inspired, and the recording more like a demo in a way – birthed and left untouched. It was definitely a development in Joni's style, having more of a minor blues tonality than anything she'd released before. As such, the song was ripe for interpretation and – befitting the Woodstock festival vibe – seemingly custom-made for the jamming style that was fast becoming rock convention.

Crosby, Stills, Nash & Young were first to release the song, their tightly-vocalised ragged rock version appearing as a single just prior to the releases of both their *Déjà Vu* album and *Ladies of the Canyon*. Their interpretation drew even more on the minor blues mode ingrained in the song. They played fast and loose with the lyrics, for example duplicating the phrase 'Billion-year old carbon' in most choruses.

Three months later came the altogether more accessible and memorable version by the UK's Matthews Southern Comfort, providing Joni with a UK number one. The more-defined chorus hook melodies clearly helped enable the single's success. The recording sounded happier than the others, more positive and less desperate to move from some state-of-being to another. Removing the negative line 'Caught in the devil's bargain' further uplifted the song's character. This version altered the song enough to challenge the theory recommending that a song is best left untampered-with essentially past its initial inspired outpouring. The changes here effectively allowed for someone else to complete the song as more suitable for the mainstream palate. The possibility was appropriate to a capitalist world caught up in commercial considerations but was, of course, a no-no for many a true artist – something Joni was considered as within the musical fraternity.

That theory notwithstanding, there was plenty of Joni's usual substance and picturesque wordplay present in 'Woodstock', the below striking image being particularly noteworthy.

And I dreamed I saw the bombers
Riding shotgun in the sky
And they were turning into butterflies
Above our nation

'The Circle Game' (Joni Mitchell)
Released as a single A-side, 1971 (JP), b/w 'Woodstock'.
Released on a four-song EP titled 4, 1971 (AU), b/w 'Big Yellow Taxi', 'Carey' and 'Woodstock'.

On Thursday 12 November 1964, the nineteenth birthday of Canadian singer/songwriter Neil Young, he wrote 'Sugar Mountain', a song that became an early B-side. The song was a lament for lost youth, reflecting his youthful desire for things, and being told 'Wait till you're older', only to discover when older that those desires had disappeared. With his teenage years about to end, he felt he'd done all he could and life's responsibilities were closing in on him. Already Joni's friend, they met again in Toronto in 1965. She heard the song and soon went about writing an answer to it. This became 'The Circle Game'.

Commenced in 1966, the chorus and first verse came easily, but Joni laboured over the rest. The remainder of the lyric eventually appeared, reflecting the need for acceptance of the inability to go backwards in life. The song was popular enough to gain two cover versions, first in 1967 by Buffy Sainte Marie, and then by Tom Rush in 1968.

Over time, the simple song came to be taught in grade three schooling in America; it's grownup subject matter viewed as a kind of nursery rhyme. It was also sung at High School graduation ceremonies. Joni was happy to see the song move into the culture in such a way. Its placement as closer for *Ladies of the Canyon* gave the album a satisfying full stop, in many ways also closing an era of Joni's music.

Blue (1971)

Personnel:
Vocals, Guitar, Piano, Dulcimer: Joni Mitchell
Pedal steel: Sneaky Pete Kleinow
Drums: Russ Kunkel
Bass, Guitar: Stephen Stills
Guitar: James Taylor
Recorded January-February 1971 at A&M Studios, Hollywood, California.
Producer: Joni Mitchell
Engineer: Henry Lewy
Label: Reprise
US Release date: 22 June 1971. UK Release date: July 1971.
Chart placings: US: 15, UK: 3, CA: 9, NO: 24

Childhood's End

Becoming famous was a huge upheaval in Joni Mitchell's life. It took her the better part of a decade to adjust to people's extreme reactions to her presence almost anywhere. It was a stress that contributed to her 1970 withdrawal from live performance. The European escape that followed yielded some of the *Blue* material, synchronised with relationship turmoil such as the breakup with Graham Nash and subsequent hook-up with James Taylor. This all led to a turning point Joni later described as childhood's end.

Recording commenced in January 1971. Joni and engineer, Henry Lewy, returned to A&M Studios on La Brea Avenue in Hollywood and locked themselves in. The new lyrics were pointed and often darkly personal. They reflected relationships, romantic or otherwise. Who the songs were about is a matter of speculation. Graham Nash has said he's not really sure if any of the songs are about him. But we do know the album was *not* inspired by American singer/songwriter, David Blue, a myth that has persisted despite Joni's attempts to dispel it. On top of all this, she was unwell at the time of recording. That could've possibly effected musical mood, but it clearly made no difference to the quality.

Stylistically, the music alternated once again between acoustic guitar and piano songs. While in Europe, Joni had taken up playing the Appalachian dulcimer, a four-stringed lap instrument. It dominated some songs, especially complimenting 'California' and its longing for a return to America. Percussion was kept to a minimum, with 'Carey' and 'All I Want' displaying the most energy. The latter and 'The Last Time I Saw Richard' were added at the last minute, replacing the slated 'Hunter (The Good Samaritan)' and 'Urge For Going'. The original tracklisting below got to a test pressing stage dated 10 March 1971.

01. Carey
02. Little Green

03. A Case Of You
04. Hunter
05. Blue
06. California
07. My Old Man
08. Urge For Going
09. This Flight Tonight
10. River

Any Joni Mitchell fan barely had time to catch their breath with the rate at which her work was evolving. *Ladies of the Canyon*, rather than signalling a more permanent shift to an experimental folk phase, can be heard in hindsight as a stepping stone. *Blue* landed on a more solid foundation, dropping the whimsical. The songs, a consistent unit, have caused critics across the decades to herald *Blue* as outstanding. For better or worse, it created a template by which to judge a lot of other people's releases. Not that *Blue* wasn't a valid yardstick, but Joni's innovation was pretty convenient for critics. For all its artistry, the album's conceptual self-adhesion made it easy to disregard some other albums if they were even *slightly* difficult to make sense of. The versatility of *Ladies of the Canyon* might've been lacking in *Blue*, but that helped make the latter so easy to pigeonhole.

In its day, *Blue* was a hit. But as the years passed, Joni lost fondness for it. Eventually, with the aid of the iconic cover shot of her by Tim Considine, the album became a benchmark, revered in its field, and a barometer for singer/songwriters of all stripes. It would be her last album on Reprise Records until 1994's *Turbulent Indigo.*

'All I Want' (Joni Mitchell)

The extraordinary opener encompasses folk, pop and jazz. It was added at the last minute as one of two songs that would replace the originally slated 'Urge For Going' and 'Hunter (The Good Samaritan)'. A light percussion bed supports Joni's dulcimer and James Taylor's intricate acoustic guitar chords which sound fresh and sparkling to this day. The instrumental changes were the right move if the goal was for *Blue* to introduce a new epoch in Joni's sound. *That* it most certainly did.

The lyric was the confession of her ability to care when it was convenient. 'Oh I hate you some, I hate you some, I love you some, I love you when I forget about me'. Like much of her work, it referred to a certain point and person in time. A quarter of a century after the fact, she didn't know what to say about the song other than to give it its due by saying it had 'more tooth' than the others.

With *Blue* now long-considered one of the greatest albums of all time, 'All I Want' can surely be considered one of its finest tracks.

'My Old Man' (Joni Mitchell)

Released as a single B-side, 13 August 1971 (UK and IE), b/w 'Carey'.

If, as many believed, 'My Old Man' referred to Graham Nash, Joni would've needed to be highly objective indeed to include the passionate song on *Blue* the best part of a year after their breakup. Wouldn't it be more logical for the lyric to refer to Joni's then-new beau James Taylor? This is one relationship aspect worthy of examination.

A lyric sketch exists on letterhead from Copenhagen's Palace Hotel, which Joni possibly visited on her European jaunt in the spring of 1970. She and Taylor would not pair up until the summer, but she could easily have carried the notepad around and used it later. A clue may reside in the sketch itself. One crossed-out line is 'Once when we were in London', which could be construed as a Nash reference. But she could've been reflecting the present through the past tense. She *was* in London in September performing the song live at the BBC Television Centre where, in her introduction, she spoke of the need for an extra verse. Verse two was as yet unwritten. This would appear to clinch it – the song refers to James Taylor. But then, using artistic license, it could be a conglomerate of experience and/or an ideal. Such can be the business of writing songs. Why would she write a lyric of adoration to the ex in the present tense when she was in the throes of a new relationship? That would make no sense. Taylor was definitely around. It's possible he accompanied her on this London trip, but we know he definitely *did* in October in preparation for their BBC Paris Theatre concert together on the 29th.

It's one of those little mysteries that could too easily cause a writer to construct theory to pass off as fact. We already know that Joni liked to leave lyrics ambiguous enough for the listener to come to their own conclusion and relate on their own terms without the need for a blow-by-blow explanation, and it's probably best left that way.

As a coda, and to further complicate the story, Taylor ended the relationship in early 1971, in or around the album's recording. This surely blew open the doors of lyrical inception, making the lovelorn emotional rips scattered throughout *Blue* a veritable cauldron of worms for the budding lyric analysis freak.

Whatever the song's conception, 'My Old Man' left us with one of Joni's most infamous stanzas.

But when he's gone
Me and them lonesome blues collide
The bed's too big
The frying pan's too wide

After the quasi-jazz piano arpeggios rolling through the bulk of the track, the consecutive staccato 8th-note coda chords were a quirky hook to finish with.

They were a sudden change into pop mode, not too distant from the mood of Carole King's 'It's Too Late', a huge hit at the time of *Blue*'s release. Or maybe the two tracks resonate due to it likely being the same piano played on both, recorded as they were at A&M in Hollywood.

'Little Green' (Joni Mitchell)

Being a most listenable major-key lullaby with a hint of melancholy around its delicately finger-picked edges didn't stop 'Little Green' from being slightly cryptic. When it was revealed in 1993 that Joni had been forced through circumstance to adopt-out a child in 1965, the lyric made a lot more sense. 'Call her green and the winters cannot fade her'. 'So you sign all the papers in the family name / You're sad and you're sorry, but you're not ashamed'. The song dated from 1966 but fit snugly into the *Blue* environment, where it would stand as a constant reminder of the situation, but also act as an artistic refusal to view the situation from anything but a positive perspective.

'Carey' (Joni Mitchell)

Released as a single A-side, 27 May 1971 (IT), b/w 'California'.
Released as a single A-side, July 1971 (US and CA), b/w 'This Flight Tonight'. US: 93. CA: 27.
Released as a single A-side, 13 August 1971 (UK and IE), b/w 'My Old Man'.
Released as an EP, 1971 (UK), b/w 'Both Sides, Now', 'Big Yellow Taxi' and 'Woodstock'.

In Greece in 1970, walking into the Delphini restaurant at Matala on the island of Crete was a surreal experience. First Joni heard a rattly old battery-operated record player on its last legs, pitching uncontrollably up and down, playing The Beatles' 'Golden Slumbers'. 'And they're playin' that scratchy rock and roll beneath the Matala moon'. Then behind the counter she beheld Cary Raditz, or Carrot Radish as he came to be known – a fiery red-headed and red-bearded man wearing a white turban. 'Let's have another round for the bright red devil, Who keeps me in this tourist town'.

Joni later claimed that Raditz was mean and picked on her. 'Oh you're a mean old daddy, but I like you'. Several days after their meeting, Raditz almost blew himself up lighting a kerosene stove. Realising his attitude could've been towards anyone, Joni wrote him the song for his 24th birthday anyway. She has said that the first draft was mean in return.

For the final cut, the overall musical mood was light and positive, even exotic with the congas and dulcimer. Additional flavour came from Stephen Stills playing both bass and acoustic guitar. Highly-rated, the song was first slated to open *Blue*, its position ultimately dislodged due to the addition of 'All I Want'. But the sound of 'Carey' was accessible, resulting in the issue of a single which reached the top 40 in Canada.

'Blue' (Joni Mitchell)

In initial assessment of the title track, many critics presumed a dedication to American singer/songwriter – and soon-to-be Joni's Asylum Records labelmate – David Blue. But the significance was deeper and more complex. On one level 'Blue' appeared to address options for coping with the emotional affliction; 'Acid, booze and ass / Needles, guns and grass / Lots of laughs'. On another it could've, at least in part, addressed a romantic relationship; 'Crown and anchor me, or let me sail away'. More believably it came across as a human working through whatever dark feelings were coming up – composition as therapy if you like.

> Everybody's saying that hell's the hippest way to go
> Well I don't think so
> But I'm gonna take a look around it though

Thank heavens for emotional disasters, otherwise this curling jazz-inflected piano discourse may never have existed to develop itself into 'Court and Spark' down the track.

'California' (Joni Mitchell)

Released as a single B-side, 27 May 1971 (IT), b/w 'Carey'.
Released as a single A-side, October 1971 (US and CA), 21 April 1972 (UK), b/w 'A Case of You'.

On Joni's European sojourn of 1970, she was clearly homesick. 'California' read like a diary entry. This time the location was France, at least in verse one. 'But I wouldn't want to stay here, it's too old and cold and settled in its ways here'. Verse two resurrected the star of 'Carey', Cary Raditz, 'The red red rogue'. 'I met a redneck on a Grecian isle'. Verse three found Joni in Spain going 'To a party down a red dirt road'. This occurred at a home belonging to *Rolling Stone* magazine founder, Jann Wenner.

But the choruses longed for the title's golden state, the bridge section symbolically expanding the idea out to encompass the United States in general through the consistently weeping pedal steel of Sneaky Pete Kleinow. The second bridge was especially poignant when at 2m:57s an echo delay was added to the pedal steel for three mere seconds, as if to emphasize an increasing amount of strangers feeding a growing homesickness – a touch of mixing class, to say the least.

Like the majority of *Blue*, the lyrics were the substance, the instrumentation existing in support. 'California', like 'All I Want', was a skilfully underplayed bed of dulcimer and James Taylor's acoustic guitar, with understated brushed drums courtesy of session drummer, Russ Kunkel. Perfect. (Chef's kiss.)

'This Flight Tonight' (Joni Mitchell)

Released as a single B-side, July 1971 (US and CA), b/w 'Carey'.

Just when you think you've got your *Blue* bearings, a surreal gear-change occurs. 'This Flight Tonight' with its low A-flat open guitar tuning brought an almost world music vibe not too removed from Led Zeppelin's 1970 rock raga 'Friends'. Zeppelin were in fact Joni Mitchell converts by this stage. Their song that references her, 'Going To California', and the album that housed it, *Led Zeppelin IV*, were recorded virtually simultaneously with *Blue*.

Even Scottish rock band Nazareth were enamoured enough with 'This Flight Tonight' to record it for their 1973 *Loud 'n' Proud* album, issuing it as a single. It made the UK top 20 and hit number one in Germany – an auspicious accomplishment for one of *Blue*'s more challenging compositions. Its transition from thinking-man's deep-cut to profit-making rock knockout was seamless.

But this song, believed to refer to Joni's time with James Taylor on the set of the 1971 movie, *Two-Lane Blacktop*, always had a nod to the commercial hiding away in its original semi-psychedelic treatment. Part of the final verse set a momentary scene where the narrator attempts to block the world out by wearing headphones, a pop song then filtering through singing 'Goodbye baby, Baby goodbye, Ooh ooh love is blind'. Nazareth highlighted those measures also, altering their style to a kind of stooge rock. When the band were introduced to Joni at A&M Studios in 1973, she was knocked out by the recording, giving her instant approval.

'River' (Joni Mitchell)

As we know, during the recording of *Blue*, James Taylor's unwanted exit was raw. So to associate this lyric with Graham Nash's departure, as many did, was speculative. 'River' moving into the culture as a Christmas song was also surprising. It's a breakup song. Christmas merely set the scene for the contemplation, which would be more difficult at that time of year. Logical. Not many Christmas songs would admit 'I'm so hard to handle, I'm selfish and I'm sad' unless they were a novelty. Expressing a wish to disappear is also usually absent from the festivities, and the implied euphemism of 'He loved me so naughty, made me weak at the knees' is a detail unassociated with the bulk of pious singalongs *I'm* aware of.

But seriously, the variation on 'Jingle Bells' woven into the piano part was a good argument for the Christmas association. There was enough emotional depth present to make 'River' one of Joni's most-covered songs, with well over 400 versions in existence to date. Plus, the recording was perhaps one of Joni's first to spawn its own spin-off culture, likely formative in the creation of future piano-based singer-songwriters like Tori Amos. 'River' really was the beginning of something. Indeed it was removed as the slated album closer.

'A Case of You' (Joni Mitchell)

Released as a single B-side, October 1971 (US and CA), 21 April 1972 (UK), b/w 'California'.

The usual suspects line up when considering who this lyric may refer to. Leonard Cohen is thought to be the main contender. But it's irrelevant. The song is universal in its expression of a partner having foibles that must be accepted if peace is to be kept. But even a specific line like 'I am a lonely painter' is clouded in metaphor by the following 'I live in a box of paints'. Painting things rose-coloured perhaps, but nevertheless sitting in the bar doodling on coasters, choosing to ignore on some level the advice of a woman who 'knew your life'. 'Stay with him if you can, but be prepared to bleed'.

'A Case of You' brought the final return of the instrumental combination that carried 'All I Want' and 'California' so becomingly – light percussion beneath dulcimer and James Taylor's acoustic guitar. And that fabulous closing chord a tone down from the home key, left the situation, like the majority of those in these songs, intuitively unfinished.

'The Last Time I Saw Richard' (Joni Mitchell)

This piano ballad closer is a good argument for the level of fiction that Joni could bring to her lyrics. The song was believed to be about Joni's ex-husband, Chuck Mitchell. Joni has admitted to inventing the song's waitress, so fact or fiction is ambiguous and again irrelevant. However, there is evidence to support Joni wishing to break free to follow her own muse.

> Only a dark cocoon
> Before I get my gorgeous wings and fly away
> Only a phase these dark cafe days

These closing lyrics were an appropriate full stop, as was the track itself, added to the running order at the last minute. The highly resonant vocal was completely appropriate to the tense lyric, and was a style that would wind itself down in intensity across the next album.

Contemporary Tracks

'Hunter (The Good Samaritan)' (Joni Mitchell)

First intended for inclusion on *Blue*, the track was dropped at the last minute. The studio version has never been released, but several live versions are available. The lyric fed into more of a post-hippie circumspection than was evident anywhere on *Blue*, and therefore was possibly considered out of character for the album.

For the Roses (1972)

Personnel:
Joni Mitchell: Vocals, Guitar, Piano
James Burton: Electric guitar
Wilton Felder: Bass
Bobbye Hall: Percussion
Russ Kunkel: Drums
Graham Nash: Harmonica
Bobby Notkoff: Strings
Tom Scott: Reeds, Woodwinds
Stephen Stills: Rock and roll band ('Blonde in the Bleachers')
Recorded in 1972 at A&M Studios, Hollywood, California.
Producer: Joni Mitchell
Engineer: Henry Lewy
Label: Asylum
US Release date: October 1972. UK Release date: December 1972.
Chart placings: US: 11, CA: 5, AU:19

The success of *Blue* had its share of negative repercussions. In 1971, *Rolling Stone* magazine took it upon themselves to name Joni 'Old Lady of the Year'. This was a low blow, the rock media turning on her mostly through lyric misinterpretation and a habit of being more concerned with vacuous gossip than music. After that, compliments from the magazine were non-existent for years.

Joni decided to leave society behind for a while, shed the guilt she felt for her opulent lifestyle, and 'get back to the garden' as she later called it. She moved to the coast north of Vancouver, British Columbia, building a stone structure that was more a reform school than a house, on 40 acres accessible only by ferry. It was there she wrote *For the Roses*.

After a few months, she was back in L.A. living at David Geffen's mansion on Alto Cedro Drive. With the Reprise Records contract lapsed at the release of *Blue*, Joni was now signed to Geffen and Elliot Roberts' label, Asylum Records.

For the Roses further developed the jazz element in the music. Engineer Henry Lewy heard jazz saxophonist Tom Scott's instrumental flute rendition of 'Woodstock', inviting Scott to the studio to play it for Joni. She was knocked out and asked him to play on the album. Adding to the new jazz overtone was bassist Wilton Felder, late of sessions with both funk multi-instrumentalist, Shuggie Otis, and jazz trumpeter, Donald Byrd.

Happy for Joni to maintain artistic control, Geffen nevertheless requested a radio-friendly song for the record. Joni obliged with 'You Turn Me On, I'm a Radio', later describing it as sarcastic, though its smooth delivery came across as anything but. Also on the radar was the Wardell/Ross jazz standard, 'Twisted'. But choosing to focus on her new material, she delayed recording the song until the *Court and Spark* sessions the following year.

The original album title was to be *Judgment of the Moon and Stars*, the album sleeve matching it with an innocent oceanside nude photograph of Joni taken from behind, with the sky replaced by a starry night in a thought-provoking Magritte-like image. The plan changed when manager Elliott Roberts exclaimed, 'Joan, how would you like to see $5.98 plastered across your ass?'. The photograph was averted to the inner sleeve. Then came the cover cartoon of a horse's behind with a speech bubble from the grinning animal saying 'For the Roses'. David Geffen refused to use it but did allow its appearance on a Sunset Boulevard billboard. In the end, Joni's simple outdoor photo portrait sufficed.

A contemplative coming-of-age record, *For the Roses* had the feel of a successful artist coming to terms with the reality of fame, adulation and the record business – an idea reflected in more than one of the songs, and a theme that would recur further down the discography.

'Banquet' (Joni Mitchell)

It would've been too easy to open the album with the obvious single choice 'You Turn Me On, I'm a Radio'. But the line 'I'm a little bit corny' might not have been the best portrayal right out of the gate, even if it *was* a metaphor or supposedly coming from the radio's mouth. The track was buried towards the album's end as it was. Instead, the prime position went to the song with the deepest sociological/ecological message.

Some get the gravy
And some get the gristle
Some get the marrow bone
And some get nothing
Though there's plenty to spare

This lyric took no prisoners with its indictment of human behaviour against the planet. 'Paper plates and Javex bottles on the tide'. 'Logs and sails and Shell Oil pails'. This was all accompanied by an appropriately drifting avant-garde piano chord progression that was never quite anchored. The final chord and melody note mysteriously landed a fourth below the given key for no apparent reason other than perhaps to emphasise the pointlessness of it all. This was Joni in the here and now, bluntly addressing the subject for anyone who cared to notice.

Considering the important message, it's surprising 'Banquet' has not been covered more in recent years. In 1975, Lani Hall – then former Brasil '66 vocalist and wife of Herb Alpert, the A of A&M – cut an essentially easy-listening version. But a more substantial interpretation came in 1986 from British progressive group, Manfred Mann's Earth Band. Theirs was a finely-wrought and dramatic affair. Considering the work they put into it, it's a shame they tamed some key lyrics as if from concern for causing some offence somewhere. That's not in the spirit of protest music at *all*.

The sheer combination of accomplished musicality and deft handling of germane subject matter surely places 'Banquet' high on the list of Joni Mitchell's foremost compositions.

'Cold Blue Steel and Sweet Fire' (Joni Mitchell)

Released as a single A-side, 9 March 1973 (UK, DE and NZ), b/w 'Blonde in the Bleachers'.

If 'Banquet' pulled no punches lyrically, the second single and its topic of heroin addiction was an even more intimidating adversary. It's as if there was an attempt to reduce the irrevocable subject down to an abstract series of inanimate ingredients or statement stills, in order to reduce their sting – a way of coping with the ideas. This was clever stuff if you consider that to merely state the obvious by exclaiming how sad, bad or mad the situation is, could be considered corny or at least predictable. Neither of those for Joni.

Red water in the bathroom sink
Fever and the scum brown bowl
Blue steel still begging
But it's indistinct

Saxophonist Tom Scott laid improvised alto lines against the bed of acoustic guitars. This timbre combination created a signature that would return throughout Joni's recordings.

'Cold Blue Steel and Sweet Fire' was an adventurous single choice for sure, borne out by a lack of chart entry. But on a purely listening level, *For the Roses* was proving to be – at only the second track in – an uncompromising, unruly, but beautiful animal.

'Barangrill' (Joni Mitchell)

Driving home late one night after a recording session, Joni pulled into a gas station. The ageing attendant asked why she was out so late. When she said she'd been at a recording session, the attendant asked her to sing something. When Joni declined the invitation, the attendant burst into an impeccable Nat King Cole impression. After two verses of 'Merry Christmas', he turned to Joni and said, 'You know, you can write a song about anything. I could make up a song about this car.', after which he launched into a whole routine on the car having nice tires and whitewalls etc.

It's an advantage to know the meaning of 'Barangrill' before you hear it. Without that, the lyric would be, not exactly abstract, but misleading. Joni herself discovered the song's meaning during the writing. Unsure what she was trying to say at first, she used the three waitresses as a spoof on the Christian trinity and went from there. The meaning of the then-unfinished song became clear to her after the gas station episode, which was retold as the song's third verse. The term 'Barangrill' was a metaphor for whatever it is you're seeking. The lyric ultimately expressed how getting wrapped up in trying to achieve can cause us to miss the beauty that's right under our nose.

The track was kept appropriately simple, with just two acoustic guitars and Tom Scott's flute and woodwind bank highlights.

'Lesson In Survival' (Joni Mitchell)

The first real piano ballad in the sequence concerned a partner's arrival into fame when you've already been through the transformation yourself. The partly abstract lyric was thought to refer to James Taylor, though it could've just as easily referred to Jackson Browne. In 1972 Joni told *Sounds* magazine, 'I had a friend at the time I was very close to and who was on the verge of tremendous success. I was watching his career and I was thinking that, as his woman at the time, I should be able to support him.'.

The lines, 'I'm looking way out at the ocean/Love to see that green water in motion', prompted the creation of Joni's naked inner sleeve shot.

'Let the Wind Carry Me' (Joni Mitchell)

The simplest, most direct *For the Roses* song yet, explored the relationship with parents and the freedom of teenage years. From the standpoint of being an adult, the last verse revealed how a continued longing for freedom always banished the pangs of desire for settling down and having children.

The rhythmically-matching backing vocal and woodwind parts are still a real treat. In fact, the track is worthy for the wind arrangement alone. Jazz harmony was taking what would become a reasonably permanent position in Joni's music. It injected an extra dimension that vanquished any remaining iota of the juvenile and laid the grounding for the arrival of *Court and Spark.*

'For the Roses' (Joni Mitchell)

The title song's topic, though perhaps not as urgent in the grand scheme of things as some of the others, surpassed them in-depth and explanation. Joni later told audiences it was about leaving Los Angeles. But it ran deeper. She saw the idea of a racehorse charging to the finish line to receive a flower wreath around its neck, only to later be shot, as a good analogy for the record business. She even told audiences the song was the first in a series of 'rejection of show business' tunes.

> Oh the power and the glory
> Just when you're getting a taste for worship
> They start bringing out the hammers
> And the boards
> And the nails

The melodic tension descending through the verse chord pattern was a clear forerunner of the Alice Cooper classic, 'Only Women Bleed', which would be recorded a mere two years later. But 'For the Roses' was all about the lyrics. One acoustic guitar and solo voice was all that was needed to get the point across. The song was Joni's farewell to show business – at least that's how she felt at the time. She would of course return, and so would the anti-showbiz tunes. Even twenty-five years later the subject still irked, the *Taming the Tiger* album mirroring *For the Roses* with a title track disapproving of the record business.

'See You Sometime' (Joni Mitchell)

This emotionally raw post-breakup song-letter to James Taylor was otherwise veiled enough to keep a listener guessing. The lines 'I couldn't take them all on then/With a headful of questions and hypes' were unclear, but could've referred to the constant press attention to Joni's personal life, not to mention the stresses the arrival of fame wrought on both parties. 'You know I'm not after a piece of your fortune and your fame/'Cause I tasted mine'. The pair had kept their relationship on the down-low as much as possible. But in 1988, Joni claimed that after mentioning Taylor's suspenders in the song, the cat was truly out of the bag when he wore them on the cover of his next album *Mud Slide Slim and the Blue Horizon.* But that record was released a full eighteen months before *For the Roses*. Unless she remembered it wrong, it's possible 'See You Sometime' was floating around her social circle for quite some time before its release.

Never one to miss a trick, in verse two, Joni forced the rhyme 'fine/lion', over-accentuating the latter word in full knowledge of her action. This mirrored the 'jew-el/schoo-el' of the virtually faultless 'For Free' from *Ladies of the Canyon.* Though the style was unusual for her, her lack of earnestness here, and willingness to not always be so purist, was refreshing.

'Electricity' (Joni Mitchell)

Firmly in deep-cut territory, the tricky 'Electricity' featured problematic fuse boards both literal and metaphorical. It dipped into social comment along the way with 'Out of touch with the breakdown of this century'. Both fuse boards and century were not going to be fixed up too easy. The clever song worked fine in isolation, but alongside fine runners like 'Banquet' and 'For the Roses', its standing was preordained.

'You Turn Me On, I'm a Radio' (Joni Mitchell)

Released as a single A-side, October 1972 (US and CA), 10 November 1972 (UK), 30 November 1972 (AU), b/w 'Urge For Going'. US: 25. CA: 10. AU: 37.
Released as a single A-side, July 1976 (UK), b/w 'Free Man in Paris'.

The first Joni Mitchell single to hit the Billboard top 40 was written after Asylum Records requested a radio-friendly song. The idea existed first as a drawing of an old Marconi radio. The song wasn't intended to be taken seriously, but the lyric revealed the general radio metaphor to be a disguise for yet another relationship.

I know you don't like weak women
You get bored so quick
And you don't like strong women
'Cause they're hip to your tricks

If your head says forget it
But your heart's still smoking
Call me at the station
The lines are open

It worked. The single, with country lilt supported by Graham Nash' harmonica performance, became Joni's first Canadian top ten hit, also achieving a number three Adult Contemporary placement there

'Blonde in the Bleachers' (Joni Mitchell)

Released as a single B-side, 9 March 1973 (UK, DE and NZ), b/w 'Cold Blue Steel and Sweet Fire'.

Like 'Electricity', this all-too-brief piano pop ballad has a lyric quirk, but this time it veils the meaning. The pronoun 'you' changing back and forth from specific to general makes it unclear who's being referred to at a given time. Is it him or is it her? 'She follows you home/But you miss living alone' is for him. But 'It seems like you've gotta give up such a piece of your soul/ When you give up the chase' is for her. And who is 'her' anyway? Some have suggested she's a groupie. But she doesn't yet seem to know that score, and comes across more like having a genuine love interest in the 'rock and roll man'.

The track has beautiful things in it, perhaps too many if you consider the function of a musical arrangement to be to coax out the song and little more. Towards the end, the bass and drums kick in, eventually breaking into a near-Latin-American feel that doesn't quite lift off. It's a good example of a constrained track bursting to break out to the freedom that *Court and Spark* would eventually sanction.

'Woman of Heart and Mind' (Joni Mitchell)

Reaching 'Woman of Heart and Mind' is the point when all the relationship shenanigans begin to feel a tad earnest and their presence in the songs, prolonged. This lyric was certainly absent of the candid sincerity that caused *Blue* to so vividly radiate. As we know, Joni clearly thought something was needed in light of the style development that the coming *Court and Spark* would foster. It's not like she wouldn't record more love songs, but after *For the Roses*, the music progressed so constantly, you could barely keep up. The lyrics then became elegantly decorated with increasing literary techniques and surprises that were in danger of rendering any subject matter as secondary. Is that not the point in consideration of a lyric though anyway, that it's not the subject but the way it's handled that matters? Having said that, we find here in verse three, an expletive.

Drive your bargains
Push your papers
Win your medals
Fuck your strangers
Don't it leave you on the empty side

It is the perfect word to make the point. No more or less required than any other. And that gorgeous augmented-11th chord to finish! Despite any perceived failing on my part (meaning the earnestness, not the expletive), this music always had elements to win you over.

'Judgement of the Moon and Stars (Ludwig's Tune)' (Joni Mitchell)

According to Joni in 1972, this lyric was from the perspective of Beethoven's muse talking to him. She said that in reading books about the composer,his feeling towards his friends felt familiar to Joni. This is most likely how the old chestnut that she compared herself to Beethoven came into the culture. Sadly, many snatch such perceptions and sprint with them. If this song hadn't been written, that misunderstanding may never have occurred.

The lyric – where the narrator attempts to give the composer confidence in the face of tragedy – underwent quite a transformation before its completion. The original title was 'Letter to the Deaf Master'. The hand-written notes still exist, showing many a crossed-out line. 'You're going to learn to drive your devil' became 'How do you learn to shake the devil?'. That too was abandoned, the word 'shake' retained for the keeper, 'You've got to shake your fists at lightning now'.

Striking touches enraged the instrumental middle section. The first, forte flutes at 2m:46s, was particularly shocking. At 3m:06s, Bobby Notkoff's angry violins also withheld no wrath. All were apparent expressions of frustration with deafness, as was the below stanza of advice.

If you're feeling contempt
Well then you tell it
If you're tired of the silent night
Jesus, well then you yell it

The piano accompaniment was complementary to the topic, but Joni tastefully employed no trace of Beethoven in her performance.

Condemned to wires and hammers
Strike every chord that you feel
That broken trees and elephant ivories conceal

Today, when clichés like 'genius' and 'masterpiece' litter like confetti, I find I must seriously consider the latter in relation to this song. It's daunting enough freestanding and was an unforeseen surprise in the context of *For the Roses*. But, to haul out another cliché; 'Hard act to follow'. The song's very presentation suggests the only sensible following recourse to surely be an abrupt direction change.

Contemporary Tracks

Urge For Going (Joni Mitchell)

Released as a single B-side, October 1972 (US and CA), 10 November 1972 (UK), 30 November 1972 (AU), b/w 'You Turn Me On, I'm a Radio'.

Completed in August 1966, the popular 'Urge For Going' originally referred to the deterioration of the folk movement. The writing came easily, but as the months turned dark, the subject matter lightened to an exasperation with the onset of the Saskatchewan winter. This made the song accessible, garnering several late '60s covers, most notably those by folk and country singers, Tom Rush and George Hamilton IV.

Joni first cut the song for *Blue* but dropped it from the proposed sequence. This was perhaps partially due to her current style development but was more likely the consequence of adding 'All I Want' and 'The Last Time I Saw Richard'. In 1967 she said 'Urge For Going' was the only song she played in standard guitar tuning.

'Like Veils, Said Lorraine' (Joni Mitchell)

This *For the Roses* outtake has never been made available. The lyric expresses life's difficulties. Fitting the title track, it also touches on the pitfalls of fame.

That wisdom and the grace
And you know you don't get that
From high finance or fame
If you're stuck in that frame
Or the paint that you put
On your face or your name

'Midnight Cowboy' (Joni Mitchell)

This song was recorded by soul singer, Donal Leace, for his self-titled 1972 Atlantic album. One or two lyric lines were updated for that recording. It's worth a listen for the dexterous bass-playing of Bill Salter, and electric piano of jazz great, Keith Jarrett, alone.

Court and Spark (1974)

US Release date: 17 January 1974. UK Release date: March 1974.
Personnel:
Vocals, Guitar, Piano, Clavinet: Joni Mitchell
Backing Vocals: Tommy Chong, David Crosby, Cheech Marin, Graham Nash, Susan Webb:
Bass: Max Bennett, Wilton Felder, Jim Hughart: Bass
Chimes: Milt Holland
Drums, Percussion: John Guerin
Electric guitar: Dennis Budimir, Larry Carlton, Jose Feliciano, Wayne Perkins, Robbie Robertson
Electric piano: Joe Sample
Reeds, Woodwinds: Tom Scott
Trumpet: Chuck Findley
Recorded in 1973 at A&M Studios, Hollywood, California.
Producer: Joni Mitchell and Henry Lewy
Engineer: Henry Lewy and Ellis Sorkin
Arrangers: Tom Scott and Joni Mitchell
Label: Asylum
Chart placings: US: 2, UK: 14, CA: 1, NO: 18, AU: 34

Court and Spark heralded the era of highly-polished and natural-sounding singer/songwriter productions that would last arguably for a decade or so before instrumental technology completely engulfed it. Of course, noteworthy albums already existed from singer/songwriters like James Taylor, Jackson Browne, and especially Carly Simon, whose records were taking on a slicker aura. It was as if a general attempt was being made to shed the '60s pop culture overhang altogether. That era's shadow was still being cast as late as 1974 – flower-power mourners clinging to their love beads for dear life. Others had welcomed the development of movements like progressive rock, which indeed was well in progress by 1974.

But when it came to pop, there was still a sore need for an update. That year confirmed the permanence of the jazz/rock fusion innovation that had been seeping in for a few years. Its trickle-down to pop was the antidote for a particular demographic that required more than a sharp burst of glam guitars or the admittedly infectious rhythms of the new soul music breed about to be branded with the disco tag. Not that Joni was considering any of that. She merely wanted her developing musical vision to morph into wiggling air molecules. But a change was necessary before that could happen. It wasn't that she longed to make a big jazz statement with *Court and Spark*, but that the groups she'd tried before didn't quite have a handle on her music's intricacies. At the time, there was still a style division between pop and jazz. As a player you were either one or the other. So it was during the album's demo phase that drummer, Russ Kunkel, suggested a jazz player could achieve the desired results.

After attending a performance of Tom Scott and his band the L.A. Express at the L.A. jazz club, The Baked Potato, Joni was sparked to invite them to play on the new album. In recording, she was thrilled to discover the musicians were naturally sensitive to the songs. Though they were jazz players, skilled in improvisation, they avoided overplaying, sticking to lines that moved in Joni's guitar parts already. This avoided the new harmonic and rhythmic character hijacking the songs.

Not everyone was enthralled with the move. John Lennon, in the first flush of cutting his *Rock 'n' Roll* album in a neighbouring A&M studio, paid a visit (accompanied by American singer/songwriter, Harry Nilsson), commenting that Joni's new music was 'The result of over-education. You should put strings on it. You want a hit, *don't you*?'.

Upon completion, David Geffen's focus was distracted, the bulk of Asylum's promotional attention going to Bob Dylan's *Planet Waves*. That album was fussed over at a studio playback one evening with Joni, Dylan, Geffen and a few others present. When *Court and Spark* was played, everybody talked and Dylan fell asleep, though Joni felt he was just being cute. Geffen's excuse was that since Joni was living in his house at the time, he'd heard *Court and Spark* through all its stages and it was no longer a surprise. According to Joni years later, even longtime allies Crosby, Stills & Nash 'Just sort of hissed and booed'.

In spite of it all, *Court and Spark*, adorned with Joni's beautifully deft illustration, was a success – number 1 in Canada, number 2 in *Billboard,* but number 1 in *Cashbox* magazine. It drew much acclaim, receiving Grammy nominations for Album of the Year and Best Female Pop Vocal Performance, eventually making sales of double-platinum.

The irony was that the album's success caused Joni's often superior '70s follow-ups to be unfavourably compared to it. But it *was* responsible for influencing subsequent generations of musicians – among them, Minneapolis musician, Prince. Joni has recalled seeing the teenage Prince at her '70s concerts in the city more than once. 'His eyes were so unusual and he'd kind of hide inside his coat.'. He used to write her fan mail at the time, with all of the abbreviated U's and hearts, stylised exactly as he would on his album covers years later.

'Court and Spark' (Joni Mitchell)

Released as a single B-side, November 1973 (US and CA), 11 January 1974 (UK), b/w 'Raised On Robbery'.

The title-track opener developed stylistically on the *Blue* title track and the *For the Roses* track 'Let the Wind Carry Me'. Joni has said her albums would usually include a song or two pointing towards the next album's direction. The similarity with the latter is no surprise considering they were both written in the same batch back in the Canadian retreat. Here, the jazz harmony grounding of the earlier track was matched by fuller instrumentation from the core group of L.A. Express drummer, John Guerin, session bassist, Wilton Felder, and Crusaders guitarist, Larry Carlton, in addition to Joni on piano.

An exotic streak characterised the lyric which was a metaphor for love appearing at the door like a wild-eyed scavenger. One specific reference was to People's Park, a contentious plot of Berkeley, California, land that was the venue for various anti-authoritarian and anti-war protests.

The lyric's emotional depth was reinforced by Larry Carlton's compelling guitar volume liquefaction. Further instrumental details enhanced the setting, including the surprise acoustic guitar entry at 1m:54s, leading to a striking dynamic ending of drums, bass, piano, guitars and chimes in an orchestra-like cacophony that was new for a Joni Mitchell record. With the two minutes and 46 seconds long 'Court and Spark', a new era in Joni's music had arrived – controversial for some, messianic for others.

'Help Me' (Joni Mitchell)

Released as a single A-side, March 1974 (US), 15 March 1974 (UK), May 1974 (CA), b/w 'Just Like This Train'. US: 7. CA: 6.

The hook-laden and self-explanatory second single, 'Help Me', became Joni's biggest hit. It appeared to reflect the then-blossoming relationship between her and drummer, John Guerin. Outside of the album hitting number one in Canada, this single achieved Joni's only other number one position, topping the US adult contemporary chart. It was respected enough to be nominated for Record of the Year at the 1975 Grammy Awards, where it lost out to Olivia Newton-John's 'I Honestly Love You' – surely, at least song-wise, a historic pop-culture infraction of a high proportion.

Joni considered 'Help Me' a good radio record but ultimately a throwaway. It was a distinguished production and might have been a commercial peak, but not necessarily an artistic one in light of what came later. But it *was* popular. Rock star, Prince, certainly liked it enough to insert a melodic and lyrical quote into his 1987 track, 'The Ballad of Dorothy Parker'.

'Free Man in Paris' (Joni Mitchell)

Released as a single A-side, July 1974 (US and CA), b/w 'People's Parties'. US: 22. CA: 16.
Released as a single A-side, 13 September 1974 (UK), b/w 'Car On a Hill'.
Released as a single B-side, July 1976 (UK), b/w 'You Turn Me On, I'm a Radio'.

John Lennon was drunk, and his October 1973 *Rock 'n' Roll* album sessions at A&M Studios in Hollywood had fallen into disarray. One of the many musicians present for those sessions was Puerto Rican recording artist and guitarist, Jose Feliciano. Frustrated, he'd taken a break and was wandering around the A&M complex. Suddenly he heard 'Free Man in Paris' wafting out of a studio doorway. Thinking it aligned with his playing style, Feliciano offered his services on electric guitar, despite the fact that Larry Carlton had already laid down a part. Joni accepted and before long, Feliciano's perfectly complimentary guitar part sat in the track. It can be heard on the left side of the stereo image, with Carlton's on the right. On parting, Feliciano advised Joni that she'd be best to use standard guitar tuning. In 2004 he remembered, 'She didn't like that. I think it put her off me a little.'.

The song itself was written on a Paris holiday Joni took with David Geffen and The Band guitarist Robbie Robertson. The lyric was a rare example of her adopting a character, albeit a real person, David Geffen. She later described it as a portrait of a company executive or anybody who was a cog in a machine. Geffen disliked the track, begging her to leave it off the album. Joni was most happy with it and its three-part vocal combination of her, David Crosby and Graham Nash. But she had doubts as to its single potential, favouring 'Car On a Hill'. Eventually Geffen softened, issuing 'Free Man in Paris' as a single, which earned a respectable US top 30 entry.

'People's Parties' (Joni Mitchell)

Released as a single B-side, July 1974 (US and CA), b/w 'Free Man in Paris'.

Side one ended with a pair of songs audibly and thematically linked. On an intellectual level, the acoustic-guitar-led 'People's Parties' appeared to address a lack of social confidence or at least incredulity in witnessing bizarre celebrity behaviour in a social setting. Specifically, the lyric recalled a real banquet where the ceiling, floor and all walls were mirrors, and the effect this had on the guests' demeanours. All chairs, tables, cutlery and plates were transparent. By the end of the night, Joni felt like she was too.

'The Same Situation' (Joni Mitchell)

Naturally coupling with 'People's Parties', 'The Same Situation' moved from guitar to piano, and a situation that could've easily developed from the prior lyric. The story's female is wary of the Don Juan character she finds herself with. The female could be Joni, but it works either way. Often her lyrics would have a grain of personal truth, fleshed-out with fiction, the stock-in-trade of many a so-called confessional songwriter. Social observation was also up for grabs, resulting in a kaleidoscopic blend of reality, opinion and half-truth for the sake of art. Perfectly acceptable. The level of autobiographical fact was a mystery, which was the point. Joni couldn't give *every*thing away; she'd paid the price for virtually doing that already.

Speaking of art and its associated choices, being confessional wasn't the only option she was prepared to sport with.

You've had lots of lovely women
Now you turn your gaze to me
Weighing the beauty and the imperfection
To see if I'm worthy

The word 'worTHY' – rhythmically stressed on the weak syllable – had a first-draft feel about it. But it was more than made up for by the 'truthful/approval' rhyme, not to mention Tom Scott's tense but elegant string arrangement. Considering John Lennon recommended the use of a string section, he would've approved, though these strings were more lushly orchestral compared to the angular psychedelia he still sometimes favoured in the early '70s.

'Car On a Hill' (Joni Mitchell)

Released as a single B-side, 13 September 1974 (UK), b/w 'Free Man in Paris'.

Convinced this, Joni's favourite track on the album, would make a good single, she fought Asylum Records on it. David Geffen finally went with 'Free Man in Paris', the song he originally wished omitted from the album completely. Like many Joni lyrics, there was an undertone here, this time neurotic, which possibly blocked its consideration for single release.

Otherwise, the snappy love song, replete with vocal hooks and Tom Scott's attention-getting brass stabs, was obvious single fodder. Like the ending of 'Court and Spark', there was a dynamic intensity, this time at the one minute mark. The central section combined the dual lead guitar of Wayne Perkins with Joni's powerful vocal chorale. One of the album's highlights, there's no doubt this passage had an influence on other artists' material, quite believably the magnificent post-second-chorus instrumental section of Alice Cooper's 'Only Women Bleed' released the following year – the second time that little bleeder has come up. (The other being in relation to the 'For the Roses' verse chords.)

To add to the emotional detail of 'Car On a Hill', Joni requested sound effects. The brief was 'Make it sound like traffic.'. This was achieved most tastefully through the understated guitar effects of the closing instrumental section.

'Down To You' (Joni Mitchell)

The album's central composition had long-reaching tentacles that pointed forwards in the discography. The 'pickup station' B section anticipated the harmonic mood of 'Shades of Scarlett Conquering' from The Hissing of Summer Lawns. So too the group vocals of Joni, David Crosby and Susan Webb (sister of songwriter, Jimmy Webb) foreshadowed that album's 'Shadows and Light'. Even 1977's magnum opus 'Paprika Plains' was foreseen in the two-minute wind and strings passage approaching the crossover third-stream jazz of American music pioneer, Gunther Schuller. Arranged by both Joni and Tom Scott, the passage was balanced and consistent but forceful in its expectations of a listener. You can understand the pure folk faction of Joni's devotees baulking at the cerebral music displayed here. Likewise, you can sense the sigh of satisfaction that must surely have expelled from others who championed her progressive exploration.

Giving a bit more leg-room, the more accessible lyric combined small talk and philosophy, underscored by colourful aural imagery. A canvas of roaming piano and a resolute strings-sustain confirmed the narrator's obvious intentions in the lyric scene below.

> You go down to the pick-up station
> Craving warmth and beauty
> You settle for less than fascination
> A few drinks later you're not so choosy

The intricate and almost disco clavinet improvisation added to that scene was an inspired detail. Hearing it quietly off in the left corner, there was no mistaking the era and location.

'Down To You' was an arresting evolution in Joni's sound, and quite rightly won her and Tom Scott the 1975 Grammy award for Best Arrangement Accompanying Vocalists.

'Just Like This Train' (Joni Mitchell)

Released as a single B-side, March 1974 (US), 15 March 1974 (UK), May 1974 (CA), b/w 'Help Me'.

The perfect follow-on from the complex 'Down To You', the comparatively light-sounding 'Just Like This Train' was in fact a song of jealousy and was purported to refer to James Taylor. Joni later claimed the line 'Dreaming of the pleasure I'm going to have watching your hairline recede my vain darlin'', was the nastiest she ever got. The line 'I'm always running behind the time' was ironic considering Joni was, by 1974, tending to be one step ahead, thinking of what was next. At least the lyric admitted that she had sour grapes – it just took too much comfort in them. But in 1996 when she walked out onto the stage of the *Late Show With David Letterman* and surprisingly launched into this song, she lingered on the receding hairline for a few extra bars, smiling, all sour grapes dissolved.

A slightly negative song perhaps, but it had its positives. Years later, a letter from a stranger claimed the line 'You can't find your goodness 'cause you lost your heart' saved his marriage after he applied the line's logic to the reality of his wife's indiscretion. This is the power of music. But where it related to Joni's musical artistry, that power was relatively in its inception.

'Raised On Robbery' (Joni Mitchell)

Released as a single A-side, November 1973 (US and CA), 11 January 1974 (UK), b/w 'Court and Spark'. US: 65. CA: 51.

Of all the *Court and Spark* tracks, the virtually rock and roll first single sat the most uncomfortably alongside its superior siblings. Why the phrase ''57 BIScayne' was weakly placed on the meter is a mystery, also considering that model of Chevrolet didn't hit the market till 1958, and to sing ''58 BisCAYNE' would've occurred more naturally in the meter. Artistic license at work.

Some distinguished guitar from The Band's Robbie Robertson did little to redeem the song's presence on an otherwise virtually flawless record. But nothing is perfect. Besides, in art you need contrast – anything that's too beautiful is barely beautiful at all.

'Trouble Child' (Joni Mitchell)

After the fact, it's too easy to apply the descriptor 'abstract' to any lyric Joni hasn't clarified by naming its subject. But this particular lid was quite tightly sealed. Interpretations vary. Some hear it as an ode to childhood, others as a lament to insanity. I steer toward temporary insanity through drug addiction. Viewed through that prism, it makes sense to me.

Joni was working with jazz musicians, who were in general known at the time for considering lyrics to be of little importance. The song was first recorded uptempo, by all reports a killer track that pleased everyone involved. Everyone but Joni, that is, who needed more lyric sensitivity and a gentler attack on the musicians' part. Some had their doubts, but the slower end result proved Joni's instinct was correct and that the song could work in another way. Without the decision to re-record, we'd be minus the impressive ten-second long-held vocal harmonies on the word 'Malibu', the length of which allowed for the glorious sprayed harmonics of guitarist, Dennis Budimir. They were a fitting closing spectacle for this landmark album that was about to take itself out with an early '50s jazz standard.

'Twisted' (Wardell Gray and Annie Ross)

Trumpeter Chuck Findley weaved his way through the modulation from the end of 'Trouble Child' in G minor into 'Twisted' in D major, impeccably. In fact, the half pop/half jazz thing was a breeze for accomplished jazz players. But the essence of *Court and Spark* was its dual-genre innovation. Not that 'Twisted' really had a foot in pop beside the novelty aspect it oozed. But it worked as a pure foil against the straight rock and roll of 'Raised On Robbery'.

The work of jazz vocalists Lambert, Hendricks & Ross had captivated Joni since the early '60s. Annie Ross had taken Wardell Gray's 1949 tenor sax solo 'Twisted' and set a lyric to it. Joni would do exactly the same with the original tenor sax solo from jazz great Charles Mingus' 'Goodbye Pork Pie Hat' when she came to set its melody to lyric in 1979. The original plan was to record 'Twisted' for *For the Roses*, but it didn't work. Some argued it was equally unsuitable for *Court and Spark*, though having recently been in analysis herself, Joni felt she'd earned the right to perform the piece. That the lyric was the confession of a clearly unhinged narcissist was irrelevant – the track brought the album to a light-hearted but distinguished climax. Two added lines of dialogue from comedians, Cheech & Chong, only helped to confirm Joni's willing self-deprecation.

'What, no driver on the top?'
'Man, the chick is twisted, crazy, poop shooby, you hear? Flip city.'

In keeping with the song's closing lyric, 'I'll have the last laugh on you, 'cause instead of one head, I got two', Joni had indeed demonstrated her comfort in the realms of not only the folk-pop to which her audience had become accustomed, but now the field of jazz. And there were no plans to depart in a hurry.

Contemporary Tracks

'Jericho (Live)' (Joni Mitchell)

Released on the live album Miles of Aisles, November 1974 (US), January 1975 (UK).
Released as a single B-side, April 1975 (US), May 1975 (CA), b/w 'Carey (Live)'.

The late 1974 live album *Miles of Aisles* saw Joni backed by the core *Court and Spark* band, the L.A. Express. 'Jericho' sat comfortably within the new musical orientation, and would benefit even more from the dazzle that fretless bass player, Jaco Pastorius, would bring to the later recording for the *Don Juan's Reckless Daughter* album.

'Love Or Money' (Joni Mitchell)

Released on the live album Miles of Aisles, November 1974 (US), January 1975 (UK).

The other new song on the live album was the tale of a Hollywood movie-star-wannabe, distracted from his ambition by the memory of lost love. Short solo highlights from saxophonist, Tom Scott, and guitarist, Robben Ford, punctuated the track. Otherwise, it seems to have lost its freshness over the years, in a way that the *Court and Spark* material has managed to avoid.

The Hissing of Summer Lawns (1975)

Personnel:
Vocals, Guitar, Piano, Keyboards: Joni Mitchell
Backing vocals: David Crosby, Joni Mitchell, Graham Nash, James Taylor
Bass: Max Bennett, Wilton Felder
Chimes: Milt Holland
Dobro: Robben Ford
Drums: John Guerin
Electric piano, Keyboards: Victor Feldman, John Guerin, Joe Sample
Guitar: Jeff 'Skunk' Baxter, Larry Carlton, Robben Ford, James Taylor
Horn, Trumpet, Flugelhorn: Chuck Findley
Percussion: Victor Feldman, The warrior drums of Burundi
Saxophone, Flute: Bud Shank
Vibraphone: Victor Feldman
Recorded in 1975 at A&M Studios, Hollywood, California.
Producer: Joni Mitchell
Engineer: Henry Lewy and Ellis Sorkin
Arrangers: Dale Oehler and John Guerin
Label: Asylum
US Release date: November 1975. UK Release date: November 1975.
Chart placings: US: 4, UK: 14, CAN: 7, AU: 62

Glamorous Misunderstandings

Meeting country singer Dolly Parton, in 1975, Joni played her *The Hissing of Summer Lawns* and was met with the quiet response, 'My God, if I thought that deep, I'd scare myself to death.'. Perhaps the grind of mainstream success and touring had contributed to the deep thinking. With the L.A. Express as both support and backing band, Joni had toured America twice in 1974. These tours produced the successful live album, *Miles of Aisles*, which reached number 2 in the US. By year-end she'd purchased a dignified Spanish home in Bel Air, moving in with L.A. Express drummer John Guerin.

1975 brought more Beatles encounters. First, on Monday 24 March, Joni went to a party on the retired ocean liner the Queen Mary, docked at Long Beach, California. The occasion was a bash Paul McCartney threw to celebrate the upcoming release of Wings' *Venus and Mars.* To the strains of the onboard entertainment – New Orleans bluesman, Professor Longhair – Joni bumped into Bob Dylan. As had happened with his electric conversion nine years before, some now accused Joni of deserting her folk roots. That change had caused Dylan no real harm. Likewise, everyone else would just have to catch on to Joni's sideways redirection. She never considered herself a folk singer per se anyway – that was merely a label, a handle some chose to pick her up by. Perhaps she and Dylan discussed this at the party. What we know for sure is that meeting spawned one song from each of them. But more on those later.

Recording of the new album began in spring 1975, work often running into the small hours. This time around, Beatle, George Harrison, was recording in the neighbouring A&M studio. In the summer, with his *Extra Texture* album almost complete, he paid Joni a visit. Knocking and entering, he said 'I just wanted to say hello'. Joni became strangely shy, which led to the two being lost for words. Awkward smiles accompanied the playback of whatever track was being worked on. Harrison then invited her next door to hear his new work. Witnesses put the strange atmosphere down to the pair being in awe of each other.

In contrast, the general atmosphere surrounding the musical arrangements of *The Hissing of Summer Lawns* was looser than usual. This allowed the musicians to stretch out, resulting in a stronger jazz harmony. Joni has described those times as being more musically apartheid. People weren't really ready for a blend of pop and jazz. Nevertheless, though *Court and Spark* had been innovative, the new album pushed the boundaries even further.

In Joni's words, the general lyric topic was the plight of the suburban housewife. 'The basic theme of the album, which everybody thought was so abstract, was just any summer day in any neighbourhood when people turn their sprinklers on all up and down the block. It's just that hiss of suburbia'. She also described the songs as portraits of unfulfilled and trapped women. The lyrics shifted in perspective from the usual first-person angle to social description, changing the pronoun 'I' to 'You'. Dylan often did this. It took the heat off by providing distance. In Joni's case, it made it difficult for some female listeners, who felt the development brought up unflattering aspects of themselves. Some thought Joni was revelling in the security of success. The inner sleeve photo of her in her Bel Air swimming pool didn't help. This all constituted a massive and surprising change for some fans. But it was a misperception. The new writing technique was merely part of the constant drive to expand on the work. Eventually, Joni was philosophical, saying in 1979, 'It was my second year in office, so it was time to throw me out of office and get a new president. It's politics.'.

The cover illustration was Joni's work – a surreal mixture of L.A. and New York with a foreground of African tribesmen carrying a long snakelike drum, reflecting of the experimental track 'The Jungle Line'.

Court and Spark had made Joni the critics' darling, but they felt the new record moved too far into jazz. Joni was mystified. She'd thought the change was subtle. Later, putting it down to the press habit of blowing hot and cold on a whim, she drew an analogy with the similar plight Steely Dan endured when their 1977 jazz-rock foray *Aja* was adored by critics, but its equal, the follow-up *Gaucho*, blown off. Joni took some relief in realising she wasn't alone in it – the contrariness was just part of the territory. But for years she carried with her the mistaken belief that *Rolling Stone* had named *The Hissing of Summer Lawns* the worst album of 1975, when in fact they'd only claimed it had the worst cover.

But none of it stopped *Hissing* hitting number four in the Billboard chart. Paul and Linda McCartney even sent a telegram of congratulations. More deserved commendation came upon the album being nominated for Best Female Pop Vocal Performance at the 1977 Grammys, oddly *after* the release of the follow-up, *Hejira.*

Upon the album's release in November 1975, Joni hit the road, joining the first leg of Bob Dylan's *Rolling Thunder Revue* tour. Over time, *Hissing* came to be considered another landmark in her discography. Prince had it played before every show on his 1984-1985 *Purple Rain* tour, also proclaiming his love for it in a major 1985 *Rolling Stone* interview. Joni felt vindicated. 'That album was called all sorts of awful names. Of all my children, that was the one that really got beat up on the playground. So for him to say that in the same rag that kind of started the war against it, was a treat for me'. Likewise, British recording artist, Elvis Costello – himself an eminent lyricist – years later singled out *The Hissing of Summer Lawns* as a misunderstood masterpiece.

'In France They Kiss On Main Street' (Joni Mitchell)

Released as a single A-side, January 1976 (US), 15 April 1976 (UK), b/w 'The Boho Dance'. US: 66. CA: 19.

The language might've become more complex and literate, but the basic theme of the album's sole single was simple – the joys of growing up in a small town in the '50s. Joining in spirit and vocal performance were David Crosby, Graham Nash and James Taylor, the latter evoking the memory of doo-wop with his wailing under the 'Do You Wanna Dance?' quote.

> Under neon signs a girl was in bloom
> And a woman was fading in a suburban room

The lyric imagery was striking, and Jeff 'Skunk' Baxter's joyful rock guitar solo gave the entire theme an edge. But it was just a false alarm, as the depth of the album's middle-class observations were about to take a stranglehold. Confronting for some maybe. But after all, this was art, not accusation.

'The Jungle Line' (Joni Mitchell)

You could call 'The Jungle Line' psychedelic. You could call it the first world-music track, which many critics have tagged it in hindsight. Some have said its rhythmic basis of a practical sample of the Burundi drummers (in reality a tape loop) was the first example of such a thing, which it wasn't. That credit goes to South African singer/songwriter, John Kongos, whose own African drumming tape loop carried his 1971 hit on UK's Fly Records, 'He's Gonna Step On You Again'.

But Joni's recording was a deeper, more cerebral creature. Again, far from being an attempt to innovate for innovation's sake, it was Joni half having fun and half pushing her limitations. The lyrics alone – carrying a Henri Rousseau surrealism headlong into a modern industrial Brooklyn – trod an individual path that was alienating for some.

Rousseau walks on trumpet paths
Safaris to the heart of all that jazz
Through I-bars and girders, through wires and pipes
The mathematic circuits of the modern nights

The instrumental track was a living breathing organism, the tape loop unevenly measured, so its rhythmic and vocal characteristics reoccurred at different points in the repeating verse pattern. The title sung over the Bo Diddley lick gave a listener their bearings whenever it came back around. But Joni's wiry Farfisa and Moog synthesizer timbres left things feeling uneasy. Relaxing into the track didn't appear to be an option. She later candidly said that for about three years, she felt as if a black poet was trapped inside her. This would eventually manifest visually for the cover of 1977's *Don Juan's Reckless Daughter*.

Surprisingly, the formidable track was covered, first as a 1983 B-side by British synth pioneer, Thomas Dolby, who will reappear later in the story. But the ultimate compliment for 'The Jungle Line' came when played in variation by jazz pianist, Herbie Hancock, on his 2007 tribute album *River: The Joni Letters*, where it was recited by Canadian lyric maestro, Leonard Cohen.

'Edith and the Kingpin' (Joni Mitchell)

Working like movie scenes, the mellow jazz approach of track three betrays the underlying danger when a pimp's homecoming event attracts the press and plain-clothed police. A coterie of females taunt Edith, despite her partner the kingpin's history of leading others into a dubious lifestyle, which we the listeners are privy to, but the admirers may not be.

The scene shifts to a hotel room. The closing line suggests possible insecurities on the part of both Edith and the kingpin when they stare eye to eye but dare not look away. Why? Let's have a guess. If he loses her attention, she might pay for it. If she loses his, he might lose *her*. It's the information left out that sucks the listener in — Joni Mitchell at the top of her game.

'Don't Interrupt the Sorrow' (Joni Mitchell)

Things get complicated now. The general understanding here is that the female is standing her ground against the male, but that's only part of the story. The Jungian analysis term, anima, is the key to understanding 'Don't Interrupt the Sorrow'. It refers to the female narrator's true inner-self making an appearance in an attempt to retain her sanity at the hands of the same manifestation in the male, though the two take different forms. She has witnessed the faltering of the male's allegiances. 'Truth goes up in vapours, steeples lean'. The guy is having a meltdown. She's having none of it and he virtually stamps his feet.

She's 'Leaving on the 1:15', and fair enough. But to interpret this lyric correctly relies on contrasting 'anima' against the key phrase, 'Vengeful little goddess with an ancient crown to fight'. When she says 'Anima rising, Uprising in me tonight', the narrator is by default admitting her own weakness, in addition to that of the male in the closing measures – 'It takes a heart like Mary's these days, when your man gets weak'.

This lyric outlines dual gender weakness and is not necessarily an excuse for either gender member to cheer-on their kin. It's a lyric not solely of sexism and its response, but of equality. Like Jungian philosophy and similar literature, the benefits are hiding beneath the surface, their advantages worth more to the discoverer when uncovered as opposed to gifted. This fine work exposes Joni as potentially even more than an exemplary poet, painter and musician as if that all wasn't enough. It's perhaps as close to the intellectual as she ever got in a lyric. But it's thorny, perhaps even a difficult first listen. For the hardcore fan certainly.

'Shades of Scarlett Conquering' (Joni Mitchell)

This arrangement's function was far from being an electric band with a string section just plopped on top for colour. The strings, guitar and vibraphone were a piece, inseparable from each other, swirling around the song like the crinoline skirt the Scarlett-O'Hara-like character wore to attract the 'stand-in boys and extra players'.

She comes from a school of southern charm
She likes to have things her way
Any man in the world holding out his arm
Would soon be made to pay

Lines like those made some of Joni's peers baulk. The cultural equality they took as read from songs like 'Both Sides, Now' and 'All I Want' had appeared to harden to condemnation-with-extended-bony-finger. They failed to consider that she might simply be stepping outside of herself and not revealing her inner thoughts for a change. But they still wanted her to and took some of these third-person characterisations as a slight. They'd boxed her in and Joni paid the price. For her to merely be good in her field wasn't enough anymore. Apparently, she was expected to toe a line now. But that wasn't about to happen.

'The Hissing of Summer Lawns' (Joni Mitchell, John Guerin)

In the age of Maria Muldaur's 'Midnight at the Oasis' and Phoebe Snow's 'Poetry Man', this sensory feast had potential hit written all over it. Possibly the easiest lyric to interpret on its namesake album, it also had a hook hiding (or hissing) in every crevice of its cruisey architecture. The repeated refrain of 'Darkness' was eminently hummable, and Joni's vocal scatting so captivating as to cause the astute listener to forget the lyric's central character was in fact trapped in a luxurious prison of her own making. The details of the situation were laid out so matter-of-fact that even the negatives were appealing.

He bought her a diamond for her throat
He put her in a ranch house on a hill
She could see the valley barbecues
From her window sill

He put up a barbed wire fence
To keep out the unknown
And on every metal thorn
Just a little blood of his own
She patrols that fence of his
To a Latin drum and the hissing of summer lawns

With no evident judgment, the title track simply laid bare the pros and cons of becoming a trophy wife. As the lyric made clear, 'Still she stays with a love of some kind, It's the lady's choice'.

'The Boho Dance' (Joni Mitchell)

Released as a single B-side, January 1976 (US), 15 April 1976 (UK), b/w 'In France They Kiss On Main Street'.

As the lyric states, it's an old romance the Boho dance – the idea that any true artist relishes the years of struggling for success, even resisting achievement. Some achieve and still resist, while others dive headfirst into the rewards of celebrity. Some of those ones then come to hold their earlier struggle and even the desire to maintain it, in contempt. These ideas are reiterated time and again in 'The Boho Dance'. The below stanza suggests success as the goal.

But even on the scuffle
The cleaner's press was in my jeans
And any eye for detail
Caught a little lace along the seams

The lady below is resisting success, or at least adopting a stance to that effect.

A camera pans the cocktail hour
Behind a blind of potted palms
And finds a lady in a Paris dress
With runs in her nylons

But the individual below secretly craves a breakthrough.

Like a priest with a pornographic watch
Looking and longing on the sly

Joni reveals her own position at the end.

Nothing is capsulised in me
On either side of town
The streets were never really mine
Not mine these glamour gowns

These are four lines that could only be written by someone with experience on both sides of the tracks, but with an allegiance to neither for the duration.

The harmony riding on the 16th-note groove is rooted in jazz, its tentacles stretching back to a kind of cool noir nostalgia and forwards to embrace the cutting edge through Joni's spidery Moog synthesizer lines. That dual concept matches the lyric's in-built opposition. In compliment, a pair of muted trumpets take the song out, cross-fading into 'Harry's House'.

'Harry's House; Centerpiece' (Joni Mitchell; Harry Edison, Jon Hendricks, Johnny Mandel)

The introductory muted trumpets fading in from 'The Boho Dance' were artificially slowed down with a pitch modulator. The instrument base shifted from piano to guitar, and the style was similar enough for 'Harry's House' to sound like a continuation.

But the lyric was a huge displacement from bohemian ideal into existential reality. The wife and kids at home 'keep their gut reactions hid' while the husband far away, takes a yellow taxi fish to a hotel, but a helicopter to a board meeting. There he drifts into a reverie recalling a teenage swimming pool rejection. At that point the track changes to a cover version of the 1958 jazz standard, 'Centerpiece', that Joni knew so well from the Lambert, Hendricks & Ross version. Pianist, Joe Sample, steals the show with a provocative solo before a clear audio edit cuts to Joni's multi-tracked vocals delivering another verse. We are then privy to the wife's side of a conversation where she makes obvious her dissatisfaction with life. The reverie is broken, the first verse's taxi-fish metaphor coming full circle, the wife ultimately reeling the husband in for a rejection.

A glorious demo made up of double acoustic guitars and vocal exists, minus the 'Centerpiece' diversion. Its character is such that it could've worked perfectly on *Turbulent Indigo*, twenty years in the future. It goes to show that these songs alone were an accomplishment, undemanding of additional ornamentation which was all an unnecessary though pleasant bonus.

'Sweet Bird' (Joni Mitchell)

Being the simplest, perhaps most easily understood piece on *The Hissing of Summer Lawns* doesn't undermine this ballad's worth or integrity. Its message concerning the unwanted onset of ageing is conveyed in a straightforward fashion.

Out on some borderline
Some mark of in-between
I lay down golden in time
And woke up vanishing

The lyric goes on to portray the sweet bird of youth as a creature basically laughing at the human misfortune. The line 'All these vain promises on beauty jars' instigates a consumerism concept that would be further explored on the '80s songs 'Fiction' and 'The Reoccurring Dream'.

No matter how you listen to it, the dual guitar/piano instrumental passage enacts a subtle prosody, behaving like life, running away ahead of you before you're ready. It's impossible to count through it without feeling you're being shunted forward.

For completists, a mix exists on Youtube with full intro minus the fade-in, and lasting twelve seconds longer.

'Shadows and Light' (Joni Mitchell)

The album is taken out with a virtual hymn, in the form of multi-tracked vocals on a foundation of Farfisa organ and ARP synthesizer played by Joni. She once spoke of a sharply-pitched vocal note among the track's many blended voices, which was impossible to remove. Upon hearing a playback, David Geffen winced at the point the note occurred. Asked by Joni afterwards if he heard a sharp note, Geffen said no. Joni said, 'Your mind may not have heard it, but your body did'.

Perhaps oddly contrasted with the rest of the album, the song continued to have an influence. In 1985 when Prince told *Rolling Stone* that *The Hissing of Summer Lawns* was the last album he heard that he loved all the way through, it was clear that 'Shadows and Light' would've been a formative track for his own multi-vocal escapades. The song's influence can be heard as late as the '90s, presiding over Prince tracks like '3 Chains O' Gold' with its otherwise theatrical 'Only Women Bleed'-meets-*Bat Out of Hell* mishmash.

At the heart of 'Shadows and Light' is a celebration of the vast emotional palette that art elicits, as conveyed in verse one. Verse two gives examples. But then suddenly, verse three comes down hard on the critic, who is 'Saying it's wrong, saying it's right, Compelled by prescribed standards'. 'Threatened by all things, Man of cruelty', 'Governing wrong, wrong and right'. For those fans longing for more personal confession, or even accusation, here they had it – more poisonous anti-showbiz barbs of the sort first launched from *For the Roses*, and it wouldn't be the last time.

Contemporary Tracks

Love Poem (Tom Scott)

Joni sings wordlessly on this instrumental track from the 1975 Tom Scott and the L.A. Express album, *Tom Cat.* One of many other artist's tracks she contributed to, it's worthy of mention due to the close relationship between the two acts.

Above: Outside London's Revolution Club, 17 September 1968. (*Alamy*)

Left: The debut *Song to a Seagull* (1968), the title of which was so cleverly integrated into the cover it was missed by many, most notably Reprise Records who mistakenly cropped part of the title, issuing the album as *Joni Mitchell*. (*Reprise*)

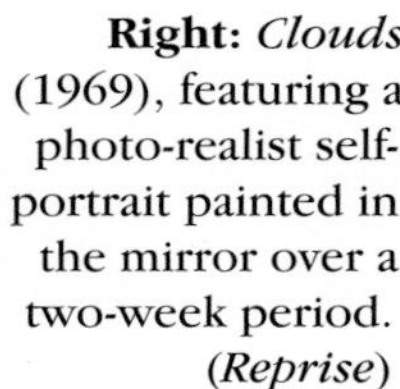

Right: *Clouds* (1969), featuring a photo-realist self-portrait painted in the mirror over a two-week period. (*Reprise*)

Right: *Ladies of the Canyon* (1970); a self-portrait line-drawing with prominent Laurel Canyon detail from Joni's window. (*Reprise*)

Left: Tim Considine's iconic cover shot for the highly-revered *Blue* (1971). (*Reprise*)

Above: Success makes its appearance. *(Sony ATV)*

Right: Performing 'Both Sides, Now' on British TV in 1969.

Below: Joni's Laurel Canyon ranch-style home of 'Our House' fame.

Right: On Bob Dylan's *Rolling Thunder Revue* tour, late 1975.

Below: Performing the newly-penned 'Coyote' at the home of Loudon Wainwright III with Bob Dylan (unseen) on guitar, 1976.

Below: Playing the same song live with The Band in the 1976 concert movie, *The Last Waltz*.

Left: The landscape shot finally used in place of a proposed cartoon horse on the cover of *For the Roses* (1972). (*Asylum*)

Right: Both cover art and music take an artful turn for *Court and Spark* (1974). (*Asylum*)

Right: A practically avant-garde city hybrid graced the cover of the startling *The Hissing of Summer Lawns* (1975), a finely-chiselled artefact that alienated some while enticing others. (*Asylum*)

Left: Norman Seeff's portrait of Joni ice-skating in Madison, Wisconsin cross-bleeds into the fine white lines on the freeway – the destination for the leaving with no blame. *Hejira* (1976). (*Asylum*)

Left: Live on the *Mingus* tour at the Santa Barbara Bowl, September 1979. Released as the *Shadows and Light* double album and video.

Right: The full band at the same concert. L-R, Lyle Mays, Joni, Pat Metheny, Don Alias, Michael Brecker and Jaco Pastorius.

Left: On the *Mingus* tour, accompanied by The Persuasions.

Above: Larry Hulst's sublime portrait from the *California Celebrates the Whales* event at Sacramento, 20 November 1976.

Left: Playing 'Amelia' at London's Wembley Arena in 1983.

Right: Playing 'Hejira' to an aggressive audience at the *A Conspiracy of Hope* benefit in New Jersey, June 1986.

Left: Multi-character costumery, with alter-ego Art Nouveau prominent. *Don Juan's Reckless Daughter* (1977). (*Asylum*)

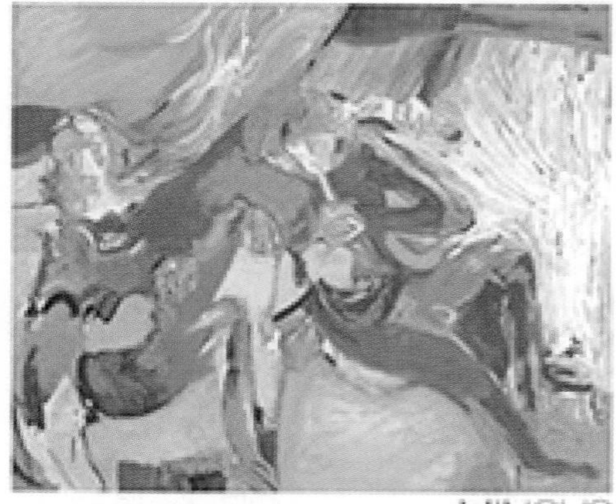

Right: Joni's abstract cover painting for *Mingus* (1979) matched the music inside. (*Asylum*)

Right: Its cover image painted from an Eric Anderson Polaroid, *Wild Things Run Fast* (1982) signalled a return to a simpler aesthetic.

Left: Joni was the prey, and the predators were the times. The '80s in full swing via the jazz-infused electronics of *Dog Eat Dog* (1985). (*Geffen*)

Left: Larry Klein's moody headshot composition - taken on a 'My Secret Place' video set – represented the popular *Chalk Mark in a Rain Storm* (1988). (*Geffen*)

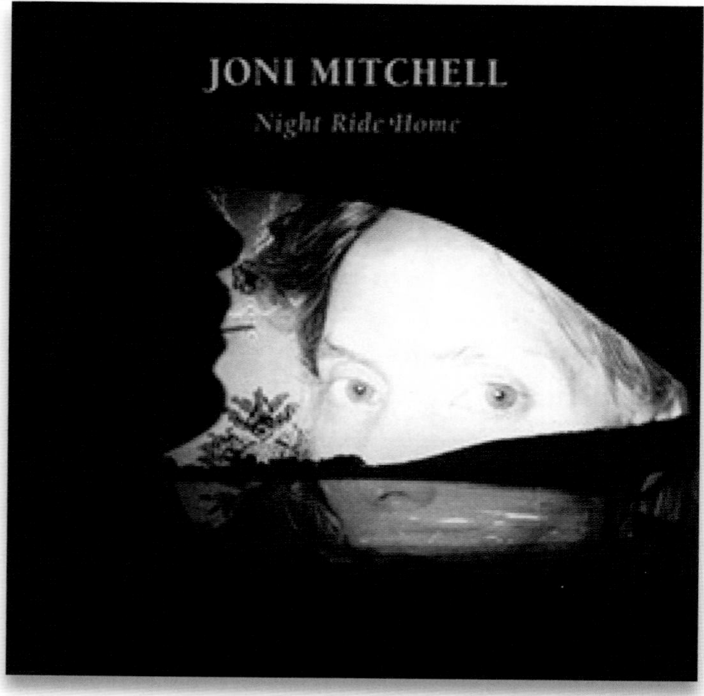

Right: Titled from the song that celebrated Joni's personal experience of Independence Day 1987, *Night Ride Home* (1991) fulfilled the return to the acoustic mode hinted at in some earlier interviews. (*Geffen*)

Right: In Van Gogh mode this time, as demonstrated in this self-portrait. *Turbulent Indigo* (1994), the hit album that resurrected Joni's status as critics' darling. (*Reprise*)

Left: With the showbiz tiger tamed in Joni's favour once again, *Taming the Tiger* (1998) followed-up the hit album with reserved style. (*Reprise*)

Left: The orchestral and predominantly-covers orientated collection that opened the new millennium. *Both Sides Now* (2000). (*Reprise*)

Right: The evocative *Travelogue* (2002) was an often astounding orchestral restatement of mostly hardcore cuts from Joni's discography. (*Nonesuch*)

Right: The primal cover shot for *Shine* (2007), taken at a performance of the ballet *The Fiddle and the Drum.* (*Hear Music*)

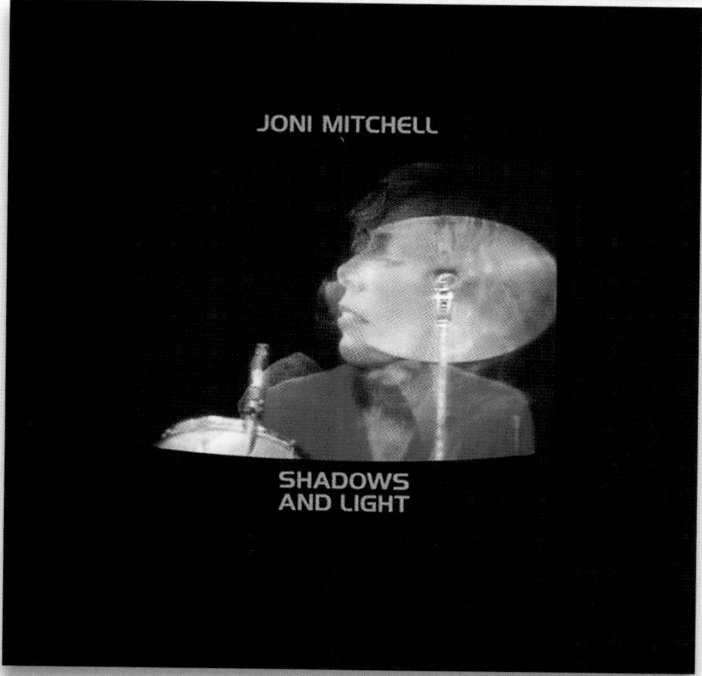

Left: The *Shadows and Light* live double album (1980).

Above: Performing 'At Last' with an orchestra on *The Late Show with David Letterman* in 2000.

Below: An emotional Joni being accepted into the Canadian Songwriters Hall of Fame in 2007.

Hejira (1976)

Personnel:
Vocals, Guitar: Joni Mitchell
Bass: Max Bennett, Chuck Dominaco
Clarinet: Abe Most
Drums: John Guerin
Fretless bass: Jaco Pastorius
Guitar: Larry Carlton
Harmonica: Neil Young
Horns: Chuck Findley, Tom Scott
Percussion: Bobbye Hall
Vibraphone: Victor Feldman
Recorded in summer 1976 at A&M Studios, Hollywood, California.
Producer: Joni Mitchell
Engineer: Henry Lewy and Steve Katz
Label: Asylum
US Release date: November 1976. UK Release date: November 1976.
Chart placings: US: 13, UK: 11, CAN: 22, AUS: 38

The USA's bicentenary celebrations firmly underlined 1976. Joni was witness to jubilees all through the South as she drove alone on the cathartic road trip that would yield the songs for *Hejira.* But a catharsis needs a precursor, which in this case had been the relationship breakdown between Joni and drummer, John Guerin. It's necessary to at least be aware of that in order to gain a true understanding of *Hejira*. The situation became unmanageable during the early 1976 winter tour promoting *The Hissing of Summer Lawns*, which ended suddenly after a Madison, Wisconsin show on Sunday 29 February. The tour remainder, including its international leg, was cancelled. This episode would loom in the forefront of some new songs and lurk in the shadows of others, like 'Song for Sharon', 'Blue Motel Room', 'Refuge of the Roads' and the monument that was the album's title track.

But the road from tour-end to album was long. It began one afternoon with Joni kicking back at Neil Young's Malibu home. Thinking she wanted to travel, she wasn't sure who with. Then two friends appeared at the door. One, an ex of Joni's from Australia, had a three-week visa to travel to Damariscotta, Maine, on a mission to retrieve his child from a wicked grandparent. The two men said they were about to leave. Joni said, 'I've been waiting for you. I'm gone'. They took off in her car to complete the mission, but she has never spoken publicly of the outcome.

Parting with her friends in Maine, Joni slowly headed back to L.A. alone, via New York, down the east coast to Florida, through the south and the Gulf of Mexico. She stayed in motels, sometimes under an alias, writing against the changing scenery as she went. This explains the absence of piano songs on *Hejira.*

Once she was back in L.A., recording began immediately. During this time, guitarist Robben Ford played Joni the self-titled debut by fretless bass virtuoso, Jaco Pastorius. He was also making noise as the new bassist for New York fusion group, Weather Report, having played on their new release *Black Market.* Knocked out, Joni called Jaco in Florida, inviting him out to L.A. to record. He cut four tracks – 'Coyote', 'Hejira', 'Black Crow' and 'Refuge of the Roads'.

Pastorius represented everything Joni dreamed of in a bass player. She longed for a certain bottom-end tone that so far had eluded her. She was bucking the current trend of bass players using dead strings, an ongoing '60s habit that had hung around far too long. She also saw no reason why the bass couldn't rise up through the mid-range notes without needing to be stuck down on the root note all the time. This request, Pastorius was born to accommodate. His performance brought radical change to Joni's music – and to think he was originally a drummer, forced to switch to bass as a teenager because of a football arm injury.

Joni loved what she later described as Jaco's 'Beautiful inflamed ego'. He'd exclaim, 'I'm the baddest. I ain't braggin', I'm just tellin' the truth'. But she did find him to be absolutely dominant. He would push his bass up in the mix, some others thinking he must be Joni's new boyfriend, but it wasn't the case. She was just powerless to control him.

With Jaco's performance representing the accomplishment of a musical dream for Joni, *Hejira* was evocative of another's leaving. In titling the album, she searched for a term meaning 'To run away with honour', finally discovering the Arabic-derived word 'hejira'. It related to the migration of the prophet Muhammad, and the concept of leaving any kind of relationship without a sense of failure.

Norman Seef's cold but undeniably elegant cover photography matched the detachment the songs strove for. Being happy to leave the dream couldn't be achieved without some skin-shedding and pain surely. The fact that the downside shone upwards through the music was unavoidable. Predictably, reviews were mixed. *Rolling Stone*'s recent icy attitude *did* begin to thaw, but some others complained of a lack of melody. Joni concurred that a more conversational jazz-improvisation approach was at the fore in preference to traditional melody. Catharsis isn't pretty. The fact that some claimed the melodies weren't easily whistled was kind of the point. It really only meant that those critics were poor whistlers.

'Coyote' (Joni Mitchell)

Released as a single A-side, January 1977 (US), 4 March 1977 (UK), June 1977 (CA), b/w 'Blue Motel Room'. CAN: 79.

'Coyote' was conceived on the road between the US states of Connecticut and Maine on Tuesday 25 November 1975. Joni had joined the first leg of Bob

Dylan's *Rolling Thunder Revue* tour and began performing an updated version of the song each night. Inspiration is believed to have come from fellow tour traveller, actor and playwright, Sam Shepard. By its completion in February 1976, 'Coyote' had a sequel titled 'Don Juan's Reckless Daughter'. The two songs were performed as a medley on Joni's US tour in January and February. But the medley was later dropped and the songs were separated, ultimately appearing on different albums.

The recording was significant in introducing the work of fretless bass player and Weather Report band member, Jaco Pastorius, to Joni's audience. His sophisticated touch secured additional visual depth, his static liquid chord harmonics mirroring the constant conveyor belt approach of the 'fine white lines on the freeway'.

'Amelia' (Joni Mitchell)

Like smooth, undulating aeroplane movement, the traditionally highly-rated 'Amelia' weaves back and forth between its two keys of F and G. Larry Carlton's crisscrossing guitar lines keep a floating sense of balance throughout, hovering over Joni's pair of liquefied guitars.

The Amelia Earhart reference feels like a eureka moment that appeared midstream, giving the composition a reason for completion. The concept ties the ingredients together – the drive cross-country, the six planes above, the well-meant advice, the lost love, and finally, Amelia's aviation resonating with Joni's emotional circumnavigation. Verse five's reference to the Greek myth of Icarus on false wings crashing into the sea, cast a metaphor for Joni's own predicament, demonstrated in homage to the myth, occupying the exact same position in the following verse.

(Verse 5)
Like Icarus ascending
On beautiful foolish arms

(Verse 6)
And looking down on everything
I crashed into his arms

She was, after all, working through a relationship aftermath, seeing parallels in the plane vapour trails and the drone of flying engines, much like Edith took comfort in the humming plane in the rain of 'Edith and the Kingpin'.

The description 'It was the hexagram of the heavens' referred to The Creative, the first hexagram of the ancient Chinese I Ching text. Its dual meaning relating to the power of both the universe and inner man was analogous to the the song's emotional journey. It also reflected the over-arching hejira concept of 'Leaving the dream, no blame'.

'Furry Sings the Blues' (Joni Mitchell)

Visiting Memphis, Tennessee, during her tour in early February 1976, Joni took the opportunity to visit Beale Street, as it was in the process of slowly being torn down. This lyric, a lament to the area's heyday, starred the character of Walter 'Furry' Lewis, an aging real-life bluesman who as a teenager lost a leg in a railroad accident. Well into his '80s, he still lived nearby in a shanty. Thanks to meeting a friend of his who recognised her in the street, Joni paid Furry a visit, an event she'd considered to be culturally impossible. As a local pawnbroker, the friend was – as the song said – chewing 'the last few dollars off old Beale Street's carcass'.

The visit with Furry was fine until Joni told him, 'I play in open tunings too.'. As if insulted, he exclaimed to the witnesses, 'I don't like her!'. This was paraphrased in the verse below:

He points a bony finger at you and says
'I don't like you'
Everybody laughs as if it's the old man's standard joke
But it's true
We're only welcome for our drink and smoke

Also included in the impressionistic lyric was the line, 'Propped up in his bed with his dentures and his leg removed', which probably didn't help, as it was later reported that Furry disliked the song.

The Memphis visit was a real step back into history, as was the song with its cast of diamond boys, satin dolls, and references to trumpeter and bandleader, W.C. Handy. Neil Young's harmonica yelps added further authenticity as if being the audio equivalent of the song's many ghosts.

'A Strange Boy' (Joni Mitchell)

The strange boy in question was one of Joni's companions on the Maine road trip. She later described the boy as 'Psychologically astute but he was just a big kid in the end.'. Their liaison played out in Maine's Newcastle Inn, where Joni played an old piano in the basement which was full of antique dolls, as described in the song. The lyric touched on love's contrary habit of beginning and ending.

See how that feeling comes and goes
Like the pull of moon on tides
Now I am surf rising
Now parched ribs of sand at his side

While the boarders were snoring
Under crisp white sheets of curfew
We were newly lovers then
We were fire in the stiff blue-haired house rules

The backing was kept as a simple bed of Joni's guitar and Bobbye Hall's percussion, topped with guitarist Larry Carlton's half-bitchy-half-pleading improvisations enhancing the whole affair. For you chord freaks, Carlton's mind-bending volumed intervals over the fade can be thought of as either a rootless Flat 10th chord minus the 5th, or a major 7th with Flat 5 minus the 3rd, slid in minor 3rds.

'Hejira' (Joni Mitchell)

Bassist Jaco Pastorius went with Joni's suggestion of multi-tracking bass harmony parts on 'Hejira', the first song he tackled. They added character to a track already brimming over with it. But without Jaco, 'Hejira' wouldn't be quite the same.

Joni has stated that the lyric was hard work. But chord-wise, this lament for the fallout of broken love is beautifully simple, certainly compared to much of her output at the time. Each verse is 32 bars long with the exception of verse two where, at the line 'Listen, Strains of Benny Goodman coming through the snow and the pinewood trees', the song takes the advice, lingering on one extra measure of E-suspended. The momentarily-heard clarinet at that point in the track came courtesy of Abe Most. Both he and Goodman had worked in some capacity with bandleader Tommy Dorsey at different times, making Most an authentic choice to play on 'Hejira' in the absence of Goodman himself.

'Hejira' is a rewarding listen, no matter how often you hear it. Its philosophy aligns more with your thinking the longer you keep a relationship with it, and its powerful imagery continues to encourage contemplation.

White flags of winter chimneys
Waving truce against the moon
In the mirrors of a modern bank
From the window of a hotel room

I know no one's going to show me everything
We all come and go unknown
Each so deep and superficial
Between the forceps and the stone

To play Devil's advocate for a moment, I suggest that some interest in the fade-out came via a mistake on Jaco's part. The end chord clashings. seesawing a semitone apart from 6m:16s, appear to stem from him forgetting to sit with Joni on the C# from that point. You can hear his initial momentary fumble up to the D note and the development he devises on the spot, continuing back and forth in and out of the clash, making a real thing of it. He couldn't possibly admit to a mistake, could he? He was after all self-proclaimed as 'the baddest'. This thinking-on-the-feet was jazz at its finest. There's always the possibility it was the plan all along, but it sure sounds like a happy mishap to me.

'Song for Sharon' (Joni Mitchell)

After the US tour imploded in the mid-west in late February 1976, Joni visited New York. At Mandolin Brothers on Staten Island she bought a mandocello and a 1915 Martin herringbone acoustic guitar. On the ferry back to New York City she began writing 'Song for Sharon' on cocaine – one of only a few songs she wrote under the influence.

The entire narrative unfolds over ten verses. The focus is on the lyrics, the band accompaniment understated and bereft of any improvisation. It would be valid to question verse one's mandolin/mannequin rhyme. Metrically stressed differently, technically they don't rhyme at all if you're being pedantic – mandoLIN, MANnequin. But in realising 'Song for Sharon' is a letter, it all makes sense. The verses stick to neither a metric pattern nor rhyme scheme but maintain enough of both to keep a listener on track — they kind of break the rules within the rules.

So, we have the acumen, but it wouldn't be Joni, without the prowess. The lyric transitions are particularly skilful. After rendering playing as a child on a bridge in Canada analogous to walking the girders of the Manhattan skyline, she paints herself as a gambler, first at bingo and then at love. Admitting she's 'a fool when love's at stake', she proves it by admitting the 18 bucks she spent on a Bleecker Street fortune teller 'went up in smoke'. So too did the relationship with the man she left 'at a North Dakota Junction' (believed to refer to John Guerin). The lyrics offer an abundance of information, but the flow is as smooth as could be.

The final verse concerns the Sharon of the title, childhood friend Sharon Bell. Of the two, it was Sharon who, as a child, entered classical competitions and wanted to be a pop singer. Joni liked the countryside and wanted to marry a farmer. 'Song for Sharon' was the vehicle to address that role reversal.

Sharon you've got a husband
And a family and a farm
I've got the apple of temptation
And a diamond snake around my arm
But you still have your music
And I've still got my eyes on the land and the sky
You sing for your friends and your family
I'll walk green pastures by and by

'Black Crow' (Joni Mitchell)

The remarkable and rhythmic 'Black Crow' is known to be a favourite of Canadian singer, K.D. Lang, and it's easy to see why. The captivating song would've made a good single. Perhaps the lack of drums stopped that idea ever holding water. Certainly, the lyric's outlining of endless travelling was accessible in a general way, and at least understandable in the extreme efforts required by Joni when exiting from and returning to her isolated British Columbian home.

I took a ferry to the highway
Then I drove to a pontoon plane
I took a plane to a taxi
And a taxi to a train

Larry Carlton's bird-like guitar effects hover around the track, striking unexpectedly, starting with that low-frequency swoop at 0m:32s. At 1m:57s, ten seconds of sharp three-dimensional echoed guitar-pick pecks squawk front-and-centre. One last energetic flurry occurs at 3m:39s, as if ravaging a carcass for the last of whatever is left – a conceptual link throwback to Beale Street in 'Furry Sings the Blues'. As in 'Coyote', Jaco Pastorius here uses sustained bass chord harmonics, effectively emulating the highway's endless ribbon. These moves show 'Black Crow' to be glancing back on *Hejira* as its end approaches.

'Blue Motel Room' (Joni Mitchell)

Released as a single B-side, January 1977 (US), 4 March 1977 (UK), June 1977 (CA), b/w 'Coyote'.

The self-explanatory 'Blue Motel Room' was written in 1976 in Savannah, Georgia, on Joni's solo road trip from Maine back to Los Angeles. It addressed relationship indiscretions, partially through the allegory of global superpowers.

You and me, we're like America and Russia
We're always keeping score
We're always balancing the power
And that can get to be a cold cold war

The track took a more mellow swing-jazz approach, with Chuck Domanico on upright bass and Larry Carlton on acoustic guitar. Joni's reverberated multi-vocal solo was a complimentary surprise dream sequence as if reinforcing the need to take stock of the situation. Indeed the lyric revealed, 'We're going to have to hold ourselves a peace talk, In some neutral cafe'.

It's appropriate to refer to 'Blue Motel Room' as a classic and a sure-fire contender for the jazz Real Book.

'Refuge of the Roads' (Joni Mitchell)

Hejira drummer John Guerin was the 'friend of spirit' alluded to in verse one of the closing track. Guerin sure reaped his fair share of *Hejira* lyric column inches, and never more intensely than in the three below lines that spell out the reason for he and Joni's breakup.

'Heart and humour and humility'
He said 'Will lighten up your heavy load'
I left him then for the refuge of the roads

I'm sure there was more to it and artistic license came into play, but leave she did – as we know, mid-tour. On her eventual way back to Los Angeles – the same trip that yielded 'Blue Motel Room' – Joni paid a visit to Tibetan Buddhist, Chogyam Trungpa, in Colorado. He induced in her a temporary state where the concept of 'I' was absent. This lasted for three days. Then what became verse three actually happened.

It was all so light and easy
Till I started analysing
And I brought on my old ways
A thunderhead of judgment was
Gathering in my gaze

In the final verse, she appeared to realise that her problems were minuscule in the scheme of things.

In a highway service station
Over the month of June
Was a photograph of the earth
Taken coming back from the moon
And you couldn't see a city
On that marbled bowling ball
Or a forest or a highway
Or me here least of all

The crash back down to earth had culminated in a real self-actualisation and spiritual achievement of the sort this entire lyric repertoire appeared to pursue. Trungpa had even shed her of her cocaine addiction. That all may be why 'Refuge of the Roads' is one of Joni's favourites of her own songs.

The instrumentation matches the substantial lyric content, largely thanks to Jaco Pastorius. He carries the recording with mostly one fretless bass part, dipping in and out of root notes, taking off to explore the harmony's further reaches. That is until 3m:41s when the first evidence of a bass overdub appears as a high register melody. From there he continues on one part again, failing to play at all for a full 18 seconds from 4m:04s. He repeats that pattern of singular bass part, overdub and silence, into the final verse, proceeding to the playout section which blossoms into four glorious simultaneous fretless bass parts. Jaco ultimately has the final *Hejira* word, ending both song and album by landing back on the starting verse chord of F, travelling full circle, just as Joni had done.

Contemporary Tracks

'Nordic Winds' (Peter Maunu)

Joni sings wordlessly on this basically instrumental track from the 1976 L.A. Express album, *Shadow Play.* She was also responsible for the album cover illustration. One of many albums she contributed to, it's worthy of mention due to the close relationship between the two acts.

Don Juan's Reckless Daughter (1977)

Personnel:
Vocals, Guitar, Piano: Joni Mitchell
Backing vocals: Alex Acuna, Don Alias, Glenn Frey, Chaka Khan, J.D. Souther
Bass: Jaco Pastorius
Drums: John Guerin
Electric guitar: Larry Carlton
Guest vocals: Manolo Badrena, Chaka Khan
In spirit: Bobbye Hall
Percussion: Alex Acuna, Don Alias, Manolo Badrena, Jaco Pastorius
Piano: Michel Colombier
Soprano saxophone: Wayne Shorter
The split-tongued spirit: El Bwyd
Surdo bass drum: Airto Moreira
Recorded January-October 1977 at A&M Studios, Hollywood, California; Columbia Studio C, New York City, and Basing Street Studios, London, UK.
Producer: Joni Mitchell, Henry Lewy and Steve Katz.
Engineers: Henry Lewy, Steve Katz, Robert Ash and Frank Laico
Orchestral arranger: Michael Gibbs
Label: Asylum
US Release date: 13 December 1977. UK Release date: December 1977.
Chart placings: US: 25, UK: 20, CAN: 28, AUS: 39

Cancelling her 1977 European tour due to exhaustion gave Joni great swathes of time to work on the new album, which would be a double. Her only live appearance that year was on Tuesday 21 June, coming on stage for the encore of a Crosby, Stills & Nash concert at Madison Square Garden. She wouldn't perform live again until her set with jazz pianist, Herbie Hancock, at the Bread & Roses Festival on 2 September 1978 at Berkeley's Greek Theater.

Recording commenced in January 1977 at A&M when Joni committed to tape the piano improvisation known as 'The Medallion'. That would become the seven-minute central section of the album's epicentre, 'Paprika Plains'. Over four performances, ninety minutes of playing was recorded, from which the section was eventually culled.

'Turning your back on America in favour of the Third World', was the gist of the album concept. Radical political tensions appeared in the guise of the 'Otis and Marlena' reference to Washington's Hanafi Siege of March 1977. A certain level of sentiment for the North American Indian was present, along with various lyrical and instrumental ethnic allusions. Also influential was Brazil's pre-Lent carnival, where Joni witnessed the streets filled with samba dancers. The cover collage photos were taken by Norman Seef, one of which featured Joni in the guise of her alter-ego, Art Nouveau.

Some slightly older songs were included – 'Jericho', first heard on the 1974 *Miles of Aisles* live album, 'Dreamland' from 1975, along with 'Talk To Me' and the 'Coyote' sequel 'Don Juan's Reckless Daughter', both conceived in 1976.

The rhythm section of Jaco Pastorius and John Guerin, used for parts of *Hejira*, was here enlisted for the whole. A number of vocalists guested, including Eagles' Glenn Frey, J.D. Souther and Rufus singer, Chaka Khan. A number of percussionists appeared, among them, Joni's new partner, Don Alias. Jazz saxophone legend, Wayne Shorter, made his debut in the discography on the track 'Jericho'. Shorter, percussionists Alex Acuna and Manolo Badrena, and of course Jaco Pastorius, were all current members of the jazz-fusion group, Weather Report. All-important too were the characteristic orchestral arrangements of Michael Gibbs that would enliven 'Off Night Backstreet' and glorify the penetrating 'Paprika Plains'.

Reviews were predictably mixed enough as to be redundant. What was important was Joni's opinion. She later came to view *Don Juan's Reckless Daughter* as spotty but a necessary part of her development, leading as it did to her coming collaboration with jazz monster, Charles Mingus.

An inevitable level of negative press criticism had become par-for-the-course, but Joni's main beef was with being misunderstood. Critics often completely missed the music's humour, preferring to paint her as a tragic figure. Whether they got the joke or not, this album had moments that were alive with humour. Joni was less embittered than philosophical, quipping, 'That's what stardom is – a glamorous misunderstanding.'.

'Overture – Cotton Avenue' (Joni Mitchell)

After an overture of six acoustic guitars and multiple vocals, Jaco Pastorius enters at 1m:45s, tentatively slapping a singular low F – a virtual octave below the bottom E on a standard four-string bass. A higher E down-slide follows, the album's arrival then announced proper with that frantic descending 16th-note arpeggio carrying energy more vigorous than almost anything he played on *Hejira*. We are now passengers on what Joni described as a journey through a dream world and a real world. The location is rural, and the lyrics anticipate dancing in the distant lights of Cotton Avenue – the historic African-American business district of Macon, Georgia. The area is known as Cotton Avenue to this day, though no street exists there by that name anymore.

This was something else again. Moving from the adventurous jazz/pop collision of *Court and Spark*, through the unsettling cruise of *The Hissing of Summer Lawns* to the hardcore *Hejira* live-wire skin-shed, we now landed at the mercy of a virtual jazz-fusion assault, and it felt *great!* It's unfortunate some couldn't hold on through that evolution to experience the brave and transcendent experimentation now on offer.

The music skipped and pranced beneath the lyric's brewing storm above, the effective bi-tonal horns (flown in from an outside source like a sample, I suspect) intruding in collage-like smoke wafting from the windows of the venue that was to set the scene for 'Talk To Me'.

'Talk To Me' (Joni Mitchell)

As much as these songs were a dream sequence, that didn't necessarily imply a lack of autobiography. It's believed this song referred to Joni's frustration with Bob Dylan barely speaking to her on the *Rolling Thunder Revue* tour. It's possible they hadn't had a good chinwag since the night of the *Venus and Mars* party on the Queen Mary in March 1975. Ironically, side two's sole track – the lengthy 'Paprika Plains' – came about as a result of Joni and Dylan's conversation that night. She has declared 'Talk To Me' though, to continue the dream story – the narrator's current status being drunk in the dance hall and coming on to somebody with no real outcome.

Speaking of talk, Jaco's fretless bass voice was undeniable here, again recorded in multiple overdubs as on parts of *Hejira*. At 2m:50s he even mimicked Joni's vocal effect uttered after the self-deprecatory line, 'I'm always talkin', Chicken squawkin''. An impulsive line maybe, but the metaphor endured after its earlier presence in the 'Hejira' line, 'I looked at myself here, chicken scratching for my own immortality'.

Joni might've seen it that way, but whatever the scratching signified, it worked. She'd scratched out enough compositions to have a glut at the recording of *Don Juan's Reckless Daughter*. 'Talk To Me', copyrighted in 1976, was one of several slightly older songs culled for the album.

'Jericho' (Joni Mitchell)

Released as a single A-side, February 1978 (US), March 1978 (CA), b/w 'Dreamland'.
Released as a single B-side, 3 March 1978 (UK), b/w 'Off Night Backstreet'.

It's a marvel to witness the variation between this studio cut and the earlier live *Miles of Aisles* version. The removal of Fender Rhodes electric piano, and replacement of standard fretted bass with Jaco's multiple fretless tracks (many in the form of harmonic chord punctuation), rendered what was essentially a love song as more cerebral and even esoteric. The strive for freedom within the bounds of a relationship somehow sounded more critical within the stark confines of the studio, minus the support of the Universal Amphitheatre audience.

The track is significant in introducing the work of legendary jazz saxophonist, Wayne Shorter, to Joni's music. The plaintive tones of the soprano sax here match the song's position in the dream story where it acts as a kind of soul-searching reverie after the 'Talk To Me' rejection. Joni described this as a kind of pledge '...to what you will do, what love is'.

'Paprika Plains' (Joni Mitchell)

Flashback to the evening of Monday 24 March 1975 aboard the Queen Mary ocean liner at Long Beach, California. The release party for Wings' *Venus and Mars* album would set the scene for what became partial inspiration for the 'Paprika Plains' lyric. Joni bumped into Bob Dylan. They sat in a group which eventually dispersed, leaving the two alone. After a period of silence, Dylan asked, 'If you were gonna paint this room. What would you paint?'. Joni replied, 'Well, let me think. I'd paint the mirrored ball spinning, I'd paint the women in the washroom, the band. What would you paint?'. Dylan replied, 'I'd paint this coffee cup'. That year he penned 'One More Cup of Coffee', while Joni eventually produced the more elaborate sixteen-minute 'Paprika Plains', both lyrics partially inspired by their conversation.

Forward to November 1975 and Joni's presence on Dylan's *Rolling Thunder Revue* tour. On this tour she had a dream that spawned the central unsung 'Paprika Plains' lyrics printed on the album sleeve. The 72 stream-of-consciousness lines were based in childhood memories of indigenous Canadian prairie folk and even included a nuclear vision. They were a companion to the seven-minute orchestral section, 'The Medallion'.

This middle section was the first piece recorded for 'Paprika Plains'. In January 1977, Joni found that after a break of almost two years, her piano-playing had taken a leap forward. She called her engineer Henry Lewy, telling him, 'We've got to go in the studio right now. For some inexplicable reason, I'm playing piano better than I have any right to be'. Entering A&M, she cut four improvised piano performances based on a beginning theme. From these, they cut away the main themes and edited together a seven-minute piece from the improvisations. This became 'The Medallion'. Months later she wrote the song itself, recording that piano part in August 1977, then inserting the seven-minute instrumental section.

But the process wasn't without its problems. Arranger Michael Gibbs was enlisted to orchestrate the song for strings and winds. Overdubbing the orchestra was fine until 'The Medallion' arrived when the orchestra appeared to be off-pitch. Since the January piano session, the instrument had been re-tuned more than once, becoming obvious once orchestral accompaniment was attempted. It was impossible for the orchestra to re-tune mid-performance, and the pitch difference was so marginal, it was decided to live with it.

The edit to the middle comes at 5m:14s. But the held orchestra chord introducing that section at 4m:48s appears to have intonation issues within itself anyway. But the liquid nature of that sustain makes it appropriate. The tuning can be considered a mere quirk of the piece, something only the pedantic might have an issue with. One person that did, was, of all people, jazz giant, Charles Mingus. Ironically, this was one element that attracted him to Joni's way of thinking and helped pave the way towards their collaboration album, *Mingus.*

The pitch issues were judiciously dealt with when 'Paprika Plains' was remixed for the 2005 *Songs of a Prairie Girl* compilation. Though actual pitch manipulation between orchestral instruments was impossible, the original session microphone placements allowed for some lowering in volume of the higher wind instruments when remixed. This seemed to do the trick, the occasional strings-line notwithstanding. The track is best experienced in this more fully immersive mix.

In writing the lyrics, Joni drew on the Dylan conversation and the unsung dream incorporating childhood memories. It fit into the album dream story with the trip to the restroom, the arriving storm, the childhood nostalgia, and the return to the dance hall where the narrator spots her admired target 'Through the smoke, with your eyes on fire, from J&B and Coke'.

Joni later claimed 'Paprika Plains' to be the most experimental and bewildering piece to work on. She approached it from many angles. As with painting, she found that a small change in one spot would cause an asymmetry, demanding the removal of something beautiful elsewhere, to restore balance.

As a welcome contrast, and almost on cue with the final verse line 'The band plugs in again', the trio of Mitchell, Pastorius and Guerin worked their way towards kicking into two minutes of driving chord turnaround repeats. On top sat Wayne Shorter's sublime soprano sax solo, leading to this beautiful long-held C feeding into the final orchestral sustain with its fretless-bass colouring.

'Otis and Marlena' (Joni Mitchell)

After a break to change from one vinyl disc to the next, what would the thinking have been behind how to follow 'Paprika Plains'? By this point, the dream story seemed to roll with the lyric punches. It could've become anything. It was a *dream,* after all. What we got was a narrative on a couple holidaying in Miami. They indulged seemingly oblivious to the fact that while they did, 'Muslims stick up Washington'. The line was unexpected and surely referred to the Hanafi Siege – a two-day standoff in March 1977 at both the B'nai B'rith headquarters and Islamic Center in Washington D.C.

Accommodating the concept, the instrumentation was kept simple – Multiple acoustic guitars, Larry Carlton's liquid electrics, and an intermittent John Guerin snare roll on the key lyric line quoted above. Don't forget the barely audible piano of French composer, Michel Colombier – his presence a luxury indeed.

'The Tenth World' (Joni Mitchell, Alex Acuna, Don Alias, Manolo Badrena, Airto Moreira and Jaco Pastorius)

Cross-fading in from 'Otis and Marlena', 'The Tenth World' took the former song's location of Miami, Florida, as the jumping-off point for the territory once referred to as the Third World. Essentially an extended percussion and vocal chant piece, it was perhaps out of place for any fans expecting a typical Joni sound, whatever that was anymore.

Though collectively improvised with guest percussionists, and vocalists (Including Jaco Pastorius and Chaka Khan), Joni's vision was for the distilling down of a variety of world cultures.

'Dreamland' (Joni Mitchell)

Released as a single B-side, February 1978 (US), March 1978 (CA), b/w 'Jericho'.

Another tribal percussion base, but with a substantial song on top. Minus harmonic accompaniment, Joni sang, and Rufus vocalist Chaka Khan, featured, in places improvising. It's a good idea to listen to the original Roger McGuinn cover version from his 1976 *Cardiff Rose* album, to get your bearings. Then you can return to this version hearing what the absent chords should be underneath.

Part anthropology, part autobiography ('Six-foot drifts on Myrtle's lawn') and social commentary, 'Dreamland' progressed in stream-of-consciousness imagery. It matched the 'cartoons and reruns' of 'Otis and Marlena' by unloading a succession of seductive commercial-icon brain implants – a conceptual concern that would magnify over time, reaching its apex with 1988's 'The Reoccurring Dream'.

The lyric's protagonist returning to New York 'In shoes full of tropic sand' officially brought the album's dream story to a close. The coming side four material was essentially a bonus.

'Don Juan's Reckless Daughter' (Joni Mitchell)

On the *Rolling Thunder Revue* tour in January 1976, in the process of writing 'Coyote' (The Sam Shepard dedication), Joni completed the song's sequel, 'Don Juan's Reckless Daughter'. Born two days apart, Joni and Sam were here depicted as twin souls – 'Eagles in the sky' and 'Snakes in the grass'. Where 'Coyote' was playful, the new song had a heavier, soul-searching aspect. Though on the surface, both songs were equally brisk, at least in their recorded renditions.

At the song's recording in 1977, it was opted for a smaller palette of percussion sounds, reflecting the North American Indian. Bassist Jaco Pastorius kept it simple with a repetitive slap-slide down the strings every measure, causing his hand and palm to bleed by the end of the take. It was a technique he would continue to use, apparently not without a level of annoyance with Joni for having first copped it for her own album.

With the album's dream journey finished, it was easy to place the USA as the geographic location of this song, not only from the American Indian references but also the lyric and melody line quote from the American national anthem, 'The Star-Spangled Banner' – 'Oh say can you see'.

'Off Night Backstreet' (Joni Mitchell)

Released as a single A-side, 3 March 1978 (UK), b/w 'Jericho'.

The commercial appeal was obvious here had it been 1973. A laid-back straight-four rhythm, simple acoustic guitar chords with a dissonant Led-Zeppelin-esque twist, and even psychedelic strings in an early-'70s Lennon style – the closest Joni ever came to such a thing. All admirable, but they rooted the track in a post-Beatles early '70s that had passed. It *was* deemed a suitable single for the British market, though sadly failed to make a dent, perhaps due to the lyric's slightly risqué relationship fare. But at least it showed Joni was still prepared to go there, for any stalwart fans hankering for more of that impassioned *Blue* darkness.

You give me such pleasure
You bring me such pain
Who left her long black hair
In our bathtub drain?

Commercial considerations aside, there was plenty to love. Jaco Pastorius' impeccably placed bass chord harmonics uplifted their moments. They provided an ongoing textural template for many musicians, possibly including Japan member and British New Wave innovator, David Sylvian, whose jazz-infused 'Red Guitar' – which could, in theory, be considered a branch of the *Don Juan's Reckless Daughter* family tree – *did* hit the UK top 20 six years later.

The presence of US songwriter, J.D. Souther, and Eagles member, Glenn Frey, on backing vocals, was a bonus – not that you'll know it was them without reading the album liner notes.

'The Silky Veils of Ardor' (Joni Mitchell)

These four verses carry a warning of the high cost of devotion in the pursuit of love. With a slightly slower rhythm, 'For the Roses' had been a similar expose on the downside of fame. The two songs could be a pair, even just for the presentation of one acoustic guitar supporting the vocal. In the case of the current song, a second guitar adds frills in spots. But they're kept in check, fitting the perceived suggestion to practice restraint in the face of possible calamitous disappointment.

Dare I propose that the lyric could've flowed better with the first verse popped down as the penultimate verse? In the spirit of this entire discography, yes I dare.

Mingus (1979)

Personnel:
Vocals, guitar: Joni Mitchell
Bass: Jaco Pastorius
Drums: Peter Erskine
Electric piano: Herbie Hancock
Percussion: Don Alias, Emil Richards
Soprano saxophone: Wayne Shorter
Horn section: Uncredited
Recorded Summer 1978-Spring 1979 at A&M Studios, Hollywood California, and Electric Lady Studios, New York.
Producer: Joni Mitchell
Engineers: Henry Lewy, Steve Katz and Jerry Solomon
Arranger: Jaco Pastorius (Horns on 'The Dry Cleaner from Des Moines')
Label: Asylum
US Release date: 13 June 1979. UK Release date: July 1979.
Chart placings: UK: 24, US: 17, CAN: 37, SE: 48 AU: 44, NZ: 27

Visiting legendary bass player and jazz bandleader, Charles Mingus, at his home for the first time, Joni walked into the upstairs room where he sat in a wheelchair with his back to her. Turning around, the first thing he said was, 'The strings on 'Paprika Plains' on *Don Juan's Reckless Daughter* are out of tune'. But she found him to be warm, understanding more by reading his autobiography *Beneath the Underdog*. In 1978 Joni told an interviewer, 'He's a romantic and very spiritual man – very eccentric with a big chip on his shoulder, which has kind of devoured him all his life. It's very bewildering this combination, but it's very beautiful.'.

Their collaboration was an outgrowth of Charles hearing strength and an adventurous spirit in *Don Juan's Reckless Daughter.* In addition, Joni appearing as an African-American man on the album cover caused him to consider her an audacious, nervy broad with a lot of balls. First connecting in spring 1978, Charles presented Joni with two ideas. One was for her to record an acoustic guitar piece with orchestra. The other was to condense American poet T.S. Eliot's *Four Quartets* collection down to street language, which he would then score for full orchestra. The answer to both was no. Several weeks later, Charles presented six melodies, titled Joni 1-6, requesting she put lyrics to them. These would prove to be his final compositions, as he was suffering from Amyotrophic Lateral Sclerosis (Lou Gehrig's disease).

Joni was given a deadline of three weeks to complete the lyrics. Mingus was pretty persuasive. She accepted the challenge but explained she couldn't just crank out songs and gave herself a month to write the first three. To be in close proximity to her new collaborator, she set herself up in an apartment at New York's Regency Hotel.

Mingus would give her a theme to work with, such as, 'This one is about the things I wish I'd done and the people I'm going to miss'. He also placed much importance on titling instrumental music, it being the one place you could make an actual statement. When Joni brought back a completed song, his first question was always 'What's the title?'.

The work was demanding, and Joni found it peculiar, putting words to someone else's melodic rhythms. But after doing a couple, she found them more natural to sing than many of her own older songs. Charles even claimed to have included some of her own musical idiosyncrasies in the melodies, which Joni was at a loss to ever recognise. There was an older, almost '40s crooning aspect to them, into which she wished to incorporate a newer, more progressive perspective.

Three of the tunes she couldn't get into and passed up. The most difficult one had a brief requiring her to adapt-in Mingus' personal relationship to God – an exercise she credited with frying her brain. In the end, four were completed along with a lyric for the Mingus standard, 'Goodbye Pork Pie Hat'.

Feeling time was of the essence, she wanted to finish the first three and get straight to the studio so Charles could hear at least some if not all of the music materialise. Going in with a strong group consisting of drummer Don Alias; bassist Stanley Clarke; and Mingus contemporary, saxophonist Gerry Mulligan, things quickly unravelled. Mingus resisted electric instruments and chose a traditional jazz arranger (Jeremy Lubbock), which Joni baulked at. 'I couldn't just be a cog in someone else's scheme. I had to continue the way I always had, in an intuitive exploration.'. The feel was there, but for Joni, there was a lack of intimacy and modernity in the performances. She cut the tracks with a few different line-ups before she had what she wanted. Some additional personnel along the way were;

Bass: Eddie Gomez
Drums: Tony Williams
Guitar: John McLaughlin
Mini Moog: Jan Hammer
Alto saxophone: Phil Woods
Narration: Dannie Richmond

One New York session consisting of Williams, McLaughlin, percussionist Don Alias, and bassist Jaco Pastorius, was unusable due to the latter's monstrous desire to make the date his showcase. Ultimately the *Mingus* band ended up as the current line-up of jazz-fusion group, Weather Report, but with Herbie Hancock on piano instead of that group's leader, Joe Zawinul. Hancock came in courtesy of an invite from Pastorius. Finally, Joni had her band, despite Pastorius being the only bassist on the project who felt no honour from being in the Mingus chair.

Things were looking up, and the project came to be blessed with moments of serendipity, mostly associated with the tracks 'The Wolf That Lives in Lindsey' and 'Goodbye Pork Pie Hat'. But the spectre of Charles' illness was ever-present, and with three tracks left to record, Joni wished to press on in order that they gained his approval.

Then in late 1978, with Mingus gravely ill, he and his wife Sue went on a sojourn to a faith healer in Mexico. Joni spent ten days there with them. Mingus' speech had deteriorated. He would say he wanted to talk about the music, but never had the energy. Joni last spoke with him in October. After his passing in Mexico on Friday 5 January 1979, she completed the album, finishing in the spring. The only track Charles never heard was 'God Must Be a Boogie Man'. Joni wrote the song to her own melody, basing the lyric on Mingus' self-analysis from his autobiography's opening paragraphs.

In cutting the album together, short, spoken segments called raps were interspersed between tracks. They came from tapes belonging to Sue Mingus. 'Funeral' was a conversation between Charles and friends. 'Coin in the Pocket' and 'Lucky' were comments from Charles. These tracks are omitted from the below listings.

With the album complete, Joni felt she'd achieved her desire to be true to Mingus while moving past formal jazz tradition to break new ground for herself. She was especially pleased with the work of saxophonist, Wayne Shorter, whose contribution was never less than integral and in service of the project ideals.

Joni was understandably confident in the album's potential jazz audience appeal but guarded concerning its possible pop perception. The reactionary new wave of groups like Devo was now well-established, and though she approved – equating the movement with the early 20th-century Dadaists – she chose to sidestep the entire thing.

Elsewhere in the pop firmament, Rickie Lee Jones had appeared – an American singer-songwriter who later came to be viewed as the first of a string of female artists highly imbued with a Joni Mitchell aesthetic. Seeing Rickie as having an original spin, Joni was more perplexed at the initial sight of Rickie's debut album cover. Not reading the name, Joni thought it was an old photo of herself that she couldn't place, panicking momentarily that her label had done the unthinkable – released a greatest hits collection.

The expected mixed reaction to *Mingus* arrived on cue but didn't fail to knock Joni aback. Critics, retailers and radio were uninterested. The one US station that did playlist it, soon changed its format to country and western. Joni was later to say, 'I hadn't realised the business had become so political, and that it would be so radically dismissed in every way.'. The music's obscurity caused some to view it as pretentious, which Joni disagreed with.

The experience was sobering, but Joni also said, 'I'd do it again in a minute'. The project had many rewards. The coincidences involved (Outlined below under their appropriate song entries) had thrilled her imagination. Quite possibly most of all was the startling unrelated coincidence occurring on the west coast at San Bruno just north of Mexico. Fifty-six sperm whales were found beached there on 1 January 1979. On Friday 5 January, the 56-year-old Charles Mingus passed away. The following day, Mingus was cremated, and the 56 whales set were coincidentally alight.

Sue Mingus later fulfilled Charles' request, travelling to India and scattering his ashes in the Ganges River at dawn. Joni made a further tribute, using one of her Mingus portraits as the album cover, and including the following verse in the liner notes.

Sue and the holy river
Will send you to the saints of jazz
To Duke and Bird and Fats
And any other saints you have

'Happy Birthday 1975' (Mildred J. Hill (Music))

An appropriate introduction, this one-minute singalong was an ambient recording from Mingus' 53rd birthday party on Tuesday 22 April 1975.

'God Must Be a Boogie Man' (Joni Mitchell)

Released as a single B-side, July 1979 (US), 20 July 1979 (UK), b/w 'The Dry Cleaner From Des Moines'.

After Charles Mingus passed on Friday 5 January 1979, Joni made the decision to write this lyric to her own melody. Based on the opening pages of Mingus' 1971 autobiography *Beneath the Underdog*, she'd had difficulty adhering the lyric concept of his multi-level personality to any melody he'd supplied.

She cut the track with three different bands but couldn't get the surprise quality she was after. Finally, it happened effortlessly one night when bassist, Jaco Pastorius, dropped in on a mixing session. He was in the mood to play, so the two sat down there and then, nailing the song in one take. From an acoustic guitar standpoint, Joni approached the song in a manner recalling the staccato chord moves of the 'Cotton Avenue' intro, but even more abstract-sounding minus a drum rhythm to stabilize it. Even Jaco had to watch her tapping foot to stay in time. After the fact, she didn't know how he'd managed to match many of her accents, unaware of her own in-built metronome.

This was the only track Mingus never got to hear. But Joni felt he would've approved of her adaptation, which captured the mercurial aspects of his book's self-analysis.

Well world opinion's not a lot of help
When a man's only trying to find out
How to feel about himself

'A Chair in the Sky' (Joni Mitchell, Charles Mingus)

The first-written Mitchell/Mingus piece was initially recorded very simply. Despite a couple of vocal flubs – according to Joni in 1979 – Mingus loved it. But for the album, Joni opted for a more sensuous and instrumentally embellished version. The lyric dealt with Mingus sitting high in his Manhattan apartment with his thoughts and memories, realising the end of his life approaching.

> But now Manhattan holds me to a chair in the sky
> With the bird in my ears and boats in my eyes

The key point was based on a passage from his autobiography, where one of his wives-to-be asked what he would do if he could do it all over again. He replied he'd come back bigger and better than ever, ruthless, not considering love, only in it for the bucks, minus even a heart. At the bottom of the page, he said, 'And if she believed that, she never would have become my wife'.

'The Wolf That Lives in Lindsey' (Joni Mitchell)

Like 'God Must Be a Boogie Man', Joni wrote her own melody for 'The Wolf That Lives in Lindsey' – one she'd been working on before she met Mingus. Therefore of all the tracks, it is the least tied to the album concept. But she felt the wolves married easily into Mingus' inclination towards musical cacophony.

The song also fit due to its complexity, worthy of many a Mingus composition. The live duet between Joni and percussionist, Don Alias, had a structure consisting of dropped and added beats, and odd momentary time signatures. More spontaneous rhythmic exclamations than steady time, Alias was in top form to be able to follow Joni's moves. In 1983, she told *Musician* magazine, 'As raw as it was, and as technically peculiar as it was, you couldn't beat it for spirit.'.

With the track virtually complete, Joni told engineer, Henry Lewy, that what was needed now were wolves and water gongs. Lewy vowed to spend the weekend searching out wolf sound effects in the A&M library, while Joni was away in San Francisco performing at the Bread & Roses Festival. What followed was serendipitous.

One evening while on her trip, Joni encountered a drunk stumbling across the hotel lobby, snapping his fingers and singing 'Why Do Fools Fall In Love?'. Drawn to him, they linked up, both singing as they stood at the front desk. Two more singers joined in who just happened to be members of a cappella group, The Persuasions. Moving to the bar, Joni met up with her friend, musician, Tim Hardin. Discovering there was a party on the third floor, they headed up there. In the room, the same drunk that sung in the lobby came up to Joni and casually uttered, 'I have a tape of some wolves'. Surprised, Joni said, 'Oh, I'm looking for a tape of some wolves. I'll write down my address and you send it to me'. The drunk said, 'No, I mean I've got it on me'. He then produced a box of homemade tapes full of animal sound effects.

The next day, back at the studio in L.A, Joni laid the wolf tape – a long repeating loop – against the music track. The result was uncanny. The wolf howls were in key and fit the music perfectly. Left to run from beginning to end, the howls even entered in appropriate places. Back in Berkeley for the next night of the festival, Joni played the song as an encore, blasting the wolf tape as accompaniment. Appropriately, the audience howled her back on for another encore.

'I's a Muggin'' (Stuff Smith)

Technically one of the albums raps, this short refrain sung by Joni and Mingus was a 1936 jazz standard, originally written and recorded by Ohio violinist, Stuff Smith and his Onyx Club Boys.

'Sweet Sucker Dance' (Joni Mitchell, Charles Mingus)

We now stood in potential jazz standard territory. The lyric lamented the confusing quality of a love, real and present one minute, doubtful and absent the next. The lengthy track's variation came mainly from the chord pattern. The atmosphere was liquid, the instrumental texture largely unchanging, with the exception of Joni's brief vocal scat solo. Any other improvised decoration was shared among the players.

In the discussions relating to the creation of these compositions, Mingus would play his old recordings for Joni, often pointing out when someone played a wrong note. It became a habit. Presenting 'Sweet Sucker Dance' to Mingus, Joni had changed one melody note as she thought it sounded better. Then Mingus' comment came; 'You're singing the wrong note.'. Joni argued that it sounded better going up than settling on the written blue note. He said, 'But that's a square note'. Joni replied, 'Well you know, Charlie, your note's been hip so long that it's square now, and this one's been square so long that it's hip now'. With a quizzical expression, Mingus said, 'Okay motherfuck. You sing your note and my note and put in a grace note for God'.

'The Dry Cleaner From Des Moines' (Joni Mitchell, Charles Mingus)

Released as a single A-side, July 1979 (US), 20 July 1979 (UK), b/w 'God Must Be a Boogie Man'.

Unsure whether this gambling story originally titled 'Fool's Paradise' would fly with Mingus, Joni was reassured when he suddenly lit up, telling her of his system with – and years of dedication to – the slot machines.

The album's only single, it reeked of style and panache – the star of the show, bassist Jaco Pastorius' integral horn arrangement. Carried largely by drums, percussion, vocal and bass (The only instrument establishing the underlying blues terra firma), the intermittent horn stabs, arpeggios and crescendos supercharged the environment, bringing the story's casino fully tangible. It's hardly surprising – Pastorius did nothing by halves. He stayed up all night at L.A.'s Sunset Marquis Hotel writing the charts in time for the session the next day.

The lyric too brought the Circus Casino to vivid life.

He got three oranges
Three lemons
Three cherries
Three plums
I'm losing my taste for fruit
Watching the dry cleaner do it
Like Midas in a polyester suit

The narrator says the story is a drag since; 'I lost every dime I laid on the line, But the cleaner from Des Moines could put a coin in the door of a john, And get twenty for one'.

'Goodbye Pork Pie Hat' (Joni Mitchell, Charles Mingus)

The second Mingus tune Joni set lyrics to was the classic standard from his 1959 album, *Mingus Ah Um* – the only pre-existing melody she worked on. It was originally Mingus' tribute to his friend, saxophonist Lester Young, who'd died in March 1959. But the lyric didn't come easily, taking three months before it completely appeared. Mingus had continually emphasised Young's sweet personality, telling tales of his friend's early days as a tap dancer and the fallout of Young's travelling through the south with his white wife. In those dark times, many black musicians were forced to play on the chitlin' circuit or in cellars. Joni felt the lyric should contain aspects of both men's lives, reflect the difficulty around the acceptance of black musicians at the time, but not primarily be historical. The first verse came easily. How to end was a mystery.

Then, serendipity struck, again. Mingus was away in Mexico getting treatment for his illness. Joni and Don Alias were in New York. The album was almost complete, bar finding an ending for this lyric. Heading uptown one night, Don and Joni got off the subway two stops early for no reason. Up ahead they saw a group of African-American men in a circle under a bar canopy. In the centre were two boys aged around eight or nine, dancing in a modern robot-like fashion. One of the men yelled, 'Ahaah, that looks like the end of tap dancing for sure!'. Glancing up, Joni noticed the neon above the next bar down – CHARLIE'S. The concept of 'the generations' occurred to her. Like Charlie and Lester in the old days, here were two more kids coming up the street. But the topper was when Joni saw the marquee immediately above her, its capital letters spelling out PORK PIE HAT BAR. It was jazz the boys were dancing to, and inside, the bar walls were covered in blown-up pictures of Lester Young. This odd event was the final puzzle piece, retold in the song's final verse. Charlie and Lester denoted the past, and the two boys represented the future.

Musically, the arrangement style was cool, in keeping with the original. But there was, of course, sufficient modernisation through Pastorius' fretless bass sophistication (Intermittently double-tracked) and Herbie Hancock's chiming and fluttering Fender Rhodes electric piano. Saxophonist Wayne Shorter was the time traveller if you like – the audible link between the past and present.

American jazz saxophonist, Rahsaan Roland Kirk, had put a respectable lyric to 'Goodbye Pork Pie Hat' in 1976. But Joni went one step further, setting not only the melody but also the original 1959 tenor sax solo, just as Annie Ross had done several years prior to that with Wardell Gray's 'Twisted' solo (Which Joni covered on *Court and Spark*.). On the current track, Joni remained faithful to the 1959 solo, slightly rephrasing to accommodate only the occasional word. So too Pastorius, his bass stutters at the words 'Tonight these crowds are happy and loud' mirroring those of both the double bass and saxophone heard at that point in the 1959 original. Post solo, the track opened out into an understated improv extension featuring Wayne Shorter's sax and Joni's vocal scatting – centrally punctuated by her glorious ten-second-long high F vocal note, dissolving into a flawless vibrato flourish.

True to the ideal of the lyric not being exclusively historical, the philosophical take on love shone through – as it had in 'Sweet Sucker Dance' – giving *Mingus* one final gesture seemingly straight from the profound heart of *Blue* or even a blue *note.*

Love is never easy
It's short of the hope we have for happiness
Bright and sweet
Love is never easy street

Wild Things Run Fast (1982)

Personnel:
Vocals, Guitar, Piano: Joni Mitchell
Backing vocals: Howard Kinney, Lionel Richie, James Taylor, Charles Valentino
Baritone saxophone: Kim Hutchcroft
Bass: Larry Klein
Drums: Vinnie Colaiuta, John Guerin
Guitar: Larry Carlton, Mike Landau, Steve Lukather
Percussion: Victor Feldman
Soprano saxophone: Wayne Shorter
Synthesizer: Russell Ferrante, Larry Williams
Tenor saxophone: Larry Williams
Whisper chorus: Skip Cottrell, Robert De La Garza, John Guerin, Joni Mitchell, Kenny Rankin
Recorded 1981-1982 at A&M Studios and Devonshire Sound Studios, Hollywood, California.
Producers: Joni Mitchell, Larry Hirsh and Larry Klein.
Engineers: Skip Cottrell, Jerry Hudgins, Clyde Kapian, Henry Lewy
Rhythm arrangements: Don Alias, Vinnie Colaiuta, Larry Klein
Label: Geffen
US Release date: October 1982. UK Release date: November 1982.
Chart placings: US: 25, UK: 32, CAN: 33, AUS: 51, NZ: 10, NO:14, SE: 50

Be Nice to the '80s and the '80s Will Be Nice To You

The theme of the New Year's Eve party Joni attended at singer/songwriter Stephen Bishop's home going into 1980, was 'Be Nice To The '80s And The '80s Will Be Nice To You'. There was recognition that the new decade would be a difficult era. For Joni, 1979 had had its problems too with the less-than-invigorating reception of *Mingus*, plus Jaco Pastorius' behavioural issues on that summer's American tour. But the tour did yield the live 1980 album and film, *Shadows and Light*, which hit the US Top 40 album chart. The band was Pastorius; Drummer, Don Alias; Guitarist, Pat Metheny; Keyboardist, Lyle Mays; Saxophonist, Michael Brecker, and vocal group, The Persuasions. The vocal group came aboard presumably through the happenstance of their presence and subsequent singalong in the hotel lobby where Joni came upon the drunk mysteriously pre-armed with required wolf tapes. (See entry for 'The Wolf That Lives in Lindsey' (*Mingus*). Pianist, Herbie Hancock, was asked but unable to participate. Soon Pastorius too would be absent. He and Joni naturally drifted apart, their last meeting being when she stumbled on him playing solo in a New York dive and attempted to accompany him. Over time, rumours of Jaco's further shenanigans touring the world with Weather Report would filter through to her.

For five years, Joni had dealt with an obsessive fan living in bushes near her L.A. home. He even scaled the wall at times. His sister had died in a plane crash, causing him to take an emotional stake in the *Blue* song, 'This Flight Tonight'. Joni lived under armed guard during this period. She knew the individual's identity and asked his parents to intervene. Either they did, or he simply came to his senses when, two days after John Lennon's death, in December 1980, he disappeared. Joni concluded that the death might have induced a moment of clarity in the individual.

Out in the pop world, new wave and its offshoots were blossoming. The punk movement had interested Joni as an act of revolution. She saw its strength as more in a social sense, but hoped it would cause something musical to flower. In the early '80s, she felt a personal detachment in much of the new music appearing, like they were telling what they 'saw' as opposed to how they felt. Though she liked much of it, she felt the music often lacked substance. At this point, she was a fan of Steely Dan's 1980 album *Gaucho* and Stevie Wonder's single, 'That Girl'. He, in turn, was a Joni fan, having once told her that he felt they both wrote philosophical music – a compliment she found flattering.

Also enthralled with the British band, The Police, their current hit 'De Do Do Do, De Da Da Da' had become an absolute earworm and dance magnet for Joni. Now *there* was an intact band she felt could bring something rhythmic to her music. As they happened to be mixing in Montreal, she contacted them with a view to possibly getting together. But it all changed upon meeting her future co-producer and husband, bassist Larry Klein.

Now living on the beachfront in Malibu, California, working hard on her painting, Joni considered recording again. There was one final Asylum contractual obligation to fulfil, and she intended her next record to be her swansong. There was some concern the label might insist on using a producer to keep her in line. Informing them that she was heading in more of a rock direction, she was pleased when they were happy for her to act on her instinct in the usual way. Abstract jazz had lost its lustre. Now the desire was to make a more rhythmic groove-orientated record. As it happened, Geffen Records took on *Wild Things Run Fast*. Far from a swansong, it in fact became the first of a five-album deal.

The new songs were written sporadically over the preceding three years, and their recording took time. Joni wished to incorporate jazz and folk ideas. Unlike in the days of *Court and Spark,* a new versatile breed of musician had emerged who were exemplary within both jazz and rock. With Larry Klein's help, the right combination of players appeared. John Guerin again took the drum seat, but the majority of drum performances came from powerhouse ex-Frank-Zappa drummer, Vinnie Coliauta. Klein of course, handled bass duties. Guitars were split between Toto's Steve Lukather and recent Boz Scaggs band member, Michael Landau. All of the above gave the album its signature sound, not to mention soprano sax player, Wayne Shorter, who was now a permanent fixture.

Both the band and production team of Joni, Klein and Larry Hirsh, became a well-oiled machine, all ecstatic to be working together. Klein and Hirsh handled the rhythm section matters while Joni watched over treble aspects such as vocals and horns. Lead vocals were arrived at fairly quickly singing a given song four or five times, then compiling a final take from them all.

Drum machines were in vogue, and the album got some criticism for its live drums which were out of favour with the mainstream record-buying public. Some critics made a thing of an apparent overuse of the word 'love' on the record, as if it mattered. One, over-exaggerated, claiming the word was uttered 256 times. If you included the word 'loved', 70 was closer to the truth – but 20 times in 'You Dream Flat Tires' alone if you were inclined to count these things. Love as a musical commodity was in general on the outer, for now, replaced by the exploding music video medium's representation of it; sex. Joni did, however, make the concession to include more uptempo songs. She has since said that by halfway through the recordings she was, '..starting to sound like a kind of progressive Johnny Mathis.'.

Nevertheless, the album was an exploration of what love is, those that are drawn to it and those that run from it. One theme was, growing older in a young person's world. But more than anything, Joni felt that for the first time she was able to state what she described as 'an unqualified joy'. In the past, she'd get chills at the thought of actually saying 'I love you' in a song. But due to her new relationship with Larry Klein, the necessity she'd previously felt – to have faith in a faithless world – had become redundant.

On completion, four songs were left over. One was 'Two Grey Rooms' – at this point known as 'Speechless' – which was given a lyric and vocal in 1989 and eventually included on 1991's *Night Ride Home* album. One other was 'Smokin' (Empty, Try Another)' which was included on 1985's *Dog Eat Dog*.

Joni's cover painting was based on a Polaroid of her taken by friend and folk singer, Eric Andersen. For the painting, she changed her costume, adding the horses and giving a new table perspective.

This time around reviews were positive, though Joni joked that the press kept threatening her upcoming 40th birthday. The record was seen as a timely return to a more commercial sound. It generally made the Top 20, climbing higher in some countries. On the 1983 *Refuge* world tour, a younger generation of fans attended alongside the existing fanbase. That year, Joni told *The Guardian* that her ideal audience was, 'Orange cockatoo hairstyles sitting next to basic black and pearls.'. One month after the album release and within the reassuring press glow, Joni and Larry Klein married. Vinnie Coliauta was best man.

'Chinese Cafe/Unchained Melody' (Joni Mitchell/Alex North and Hy Zaret)

Released as a single A-side, 1982 (FR, NL and AU), b/w 'Ladies' Man'.
Released as a single A-side, February 1983 (UK), b/w 'Ladies' Man'.
Released as a double single A-side limited edition, 1983 (UK), b/w 'Ladies' Man', 'The Interview' and 'The Competition'.
Released as a 12" and CD single B-side, 1988 (UK and DE), b/w 'My Secret Place', 'Number One' and 'Good Friends'.

The album opener and second single (Europe and Australia only) was a return to both autobiography and the flashback nostalgia technique. In the current case, it was nostalgia for sitting in cafes as a teenager, dropping coins in a jukebox. The first two choruses ended with quotes from Alex North and Hy Zaret's 'Unchained Melody' and Gerry Goffin and Carole King's 'Will You Still Love Me Tomorrow?', respectively. The third and final chorus broke into an entire verse of the former, leading to the ending fade.

Melancholy in mood, the song lamented the passage of time. It spoke directly to Joni's old friend, Carol, whose children were now haunting the same teenage venues as their mother. One daughter in particular now appeared to be her mother's doppelganger, despite their dissimilarity in younger years. 'We look like our mothers did now, when we were those kids' age'.

'Unchained Melody' had addressed time moving so slowly. 'Chinese Cafe' stressed its insistence on moving faster the older you get. The older song's entire first-verse quote did slow down the pace here somewhat, seeming initially like an overstatement. But taken in the context of the flashback technique, which Joni equated to inserting old newsreel clips into a movie, it made sense and created more interest.

Considering the powerhouse line-up of drummer John Guerin, bassist Larry Klein, Toto guitarist Steve Lukather, and session keyboardist Larry Williams, you might expect a showcase of sorts. But the group was as disciplined as could be, the most instrumental character coming from Klein's liquid bass-chorus effect.

The single listed 'Chinese Cafe' and 'Unchained Melody' separately, even labelling them track numbers 1 and 2, presumably for copyright reasons. The second disc of the double single had a track titled, 'The Interview', which was Joni in conversation with Richard Stanley on BBC 1. 'The Competition' wasn't a song, but simply a promo giving information on how answering six questions correctly won you a signed copy of the album with a cover art print.

'Wild Things Run Fast' (Joni Mitchell)

Like the wild male thing running from the lyric's burgeoning relationship, the title track vignette virtually no sooner appeared than it was gone. The contrast with the opening track was great. The only line up difference was drummer, Vinnie Coliauta, here making his debut on a Joni record. Though the soothing 'Chinese Cafe' was not the best style comparison, in general compared to John Guerin, Coliauta's playing was ablaze. Here he played with the same rhythmic consistency and vitality with which he'd recently set alight Frank Zappa's *Joe's Garage* and Gino Vannelli's *Nightwalker.* The approach was mostly rock, moving through more broken-down feels as it progressed – the bridge collapsing further into a ska feel reflecting Joni's love for the work of Police drummer Stewart Copeland.

Guitarist Steve Lukather made his presence more obviously felt here with that unmistakeable vibrato, winding in and out like the last verse's escape road.

All-in-all, it's quite a band and probably the tightest and most forceful collective rock playing we'd heard since *Court and Spark*.

'Ladies' Man' (Joni Mitchell)

Released as a single B-side, 1982 (NL), b/w 'Chinese Cafe/Unchained Melody'.
Released as a single B-side, February 1983 (UK), b/w 'Chinese Cafe/Unchained Melody'.
Released as a double single B-side limited edition, 1983 (UK), b/w 'Chinese Cafe/Unchained Melody', 'The Interview' and 'The Competition'.

This ladies' man – with even fewer scruples than the title track's wild male running away – is equally a commitment-phobe, with every excuse under the sun, from judgement to drug use. Drummer Vinnie Coliauta's funky 16th feel takes the heat off, as does Larry Carlton's comforting guitar tone sounding every bit characteristic of his stunning album that year, *Sleepwalk*.

The stone-cold duplication of the famous Rolling Stones lyric line, 'I'm so hot for you and you're so cold', is a fascinating detail. Their recent hit 'She's So Cold' was still in the zeitgeist as it were. The line seems less a direct reference or flashback than an unconscious remembrance. Either way, it adds to the album's open and unpretentious nature.

'Moon at the Window' (Joni Mitchell)

The swing jazz rhythm is light, the predominant harmonic mood overcast. But a level of hopelessness in this lyric can't stop the ultimate positive attitude – 'At least the moon at the window, the thieves left that behind'. It's a song Joni always felt deserved more attention. There are details aplenty to support that idea, from keyboardist Russell Ferrante's dynamic synth swells to Wayne Shorter's flittering and cawing arpeggios – the latter a sonic template that would continue on through the discography. Bassist Larry Klein's overdubs and creative string harmonics here invoke the sonic ghost of Jaco Pastorius, who was at this time on tour in Japan – the very place where the 18th-century Japanese Buddhist monk and poet, Ryokan, wrote the haiku, 'The Thief Left It Behind'.

> The thief left it behind:
> The moon
> At my window

'Solid Love' (Joni Mitchell)

Why this ecstatic lilt wasn't a single is anybody's guess. It's quite possibly the most direct and accessible love song Joni ever wrote. Though the album, in general, didn't reflect its time, 'Solid Love' spilled over with a rhythmic ska/reggae hybrid the likes of which The Police were then satiating the world's singles charts with. Open-G guitar tuning never fails to sound uplifting, and

Mike Landau's conventional intro picking here turned to Andy-Summers-Police-style splendour once an echo delay was slapped on it. Maybe it even resembled U2's The Edge, if that sells it to you better. The hit that never was.

'Be Cool' (Joni Mitchell)

Released as a single B-side, February 1983 (US), April 1983 (CA), b/w 'Underneath the Streetlight'.

The sultry 'Be Cool' was the only track cut at Hollywood's Devonshire Sound Studios. It also appears to be the first track since 'Paprika Plains' with a tuning issue, in this case the synthesizer, which plays havoc with Joni's electric guitar part. There's always a reason for these things, often aesthetic or intellectual. Maybe it was a subtle reflection of the lyric's warning against any outpouring of unnecessary emotional tension – the sharply-pitched synthesizer showing the struggle to keep a lid on it. I'll justify it that way.

'(You're So Square) Baby, I Don't Care' (Jerry Leiber, Mike Stoller)

Released as a single A-side, November 1982 (US), 19 November 1982 (UK), December 1982 (CA), b/w 'Love'. US: 47.

Sandwiched between purely contemporary intro and outro arrangements is a straight-ahead rock take on the Elvis Presley/Buddy Holly classic penned by Leiber and Stoller. It was likely chosen as a single to integrate into the then-current '50s resurgence. It worked, achieving Joni's highest US singles chart position in eight years.

Joni gave the lyric an update, with the exception of the line in parentheses.

You don't like greasy diners
You don't like sleazy bands

You don't like going to parties
To toot and talk all night long
(You just wanna park where it's nice and dark)
And kiss me sweet and strong

Of note are drummer Vinnie Coliauta's flamboyant and dexterous fills – not to mention the immaculate precision of his closing 16th shuffle, equally matched by bassist Klein.

'You Dream Flat Tires' (Joni Mitchell)

The Eagles' Don Henley was the originally chosen male vocalist for this song. But in search of an audible male/female contrast, Joni found their voices to be too similar in the melody's particular register. Dissatisfied, she called on the Commodores' Lionel Richie, who was recording across the hall at A&M. But she innocently forgot to inform Henley of the switch, which left him scratching his head when the album came out. It came up again six years later when he was asked to sing on the *Chalk Mark in a Rain Storm* track, 'Snakes and Ladders'. Mortified at the faux pas, Joni was then able to clarify and smooth things over.

One of the first *Wild Things Run Fast* songs written, the lyric examined the fear of loving – a recurring theme on the record. The motor vehicle metaphors were fresh, sparkling, and perhaps even punning for those with an open sense of humour.

With a jack and a spare you're there
Trying to get to where love is
Coming in on a rim and a prayer

The three-voice intro chords played in harmony by Klein, Mitchell and guitarist Mike Landau, touched on a contemporary percussive King Crimson texture. It threw *Wild Things Run Fast* momentarily back into that fusion whirlwind that those of us who were fans of the development hadn't quite had enough of. But the pleasant surprise would effectively be the style's swansong where Joni Mitchell records were concerned. Indeed, jazz/rock fusion *itself* had reached its zenith and was about to splinter out into corporate sub-categories like smooth jazz and eventually acid jazz and nu-jazz. But the classic period for fusion can be classified as lasting roughly from around 1969-1983, after which it became shiny and over-electronic, at least for a time. Fine fusion examples have of course endured and continue to be created, but 'You Dream Flat Tires' can be thought of as perhaps one of the last pure utterances by an original proponent within a mainstream pop context.

'Man to Man' (Joni Mitchell)

The first live performance of 'Man To Man' occurred at the Berkeley Festival, according to a 1983 Joni interview, which would place the song as existing as early as 1980. At this gig, the audience let out an audible gasp at the line, 'I sure can be phony when I get scared'. The reaction caused Joni – previously uncertain of the line's worth – to realise it must be kept in. Some fans were still taking her lyrics literally and seriously. But the decision to retain the line was for the benefit of those listeners that saw something of themselves in it.

I don't like to lie
But I sure can be phony when I get scared
I put my nose up in the air
Stoney, stoney when I get scared

The lyric's self-analysis was typical of Joni's love songs. There was a level of autobiography, certainly if you consider the line, 'A lot of good guys gone through my door'. Three of them were playing on the track! – Guerin, Klein, and James Taylor on backing vocals. Taylor and Joni's three-part harmonies panning from side to side were lustrous. Mature adults all working together, at the dawn of perhaps the 20th century's most immature decade of all – a theme that would resonate on the next album, *Dog Eat Dog*.

'Underneath the Streetlight' (Joni Mitchell)

Released as a single A-side, February 1983 (US), April 1983 (CA), b/w 'Be Cool'.

There's no doubt this track was good single fodder for 1982, despite its lack of chart appearance. It couldn't be simpler – a smooth intro leads to one section subdivided into an effective verse and chorus, stated four times with a short coda, and that's it. No musical filler and no solos. The verses start in straight brisk 4/4 rock time, but all drop to half-time after four bars, as if interrupted by the joyous vocal. The narrator – clearly in love – just can't hold all the information in. The lyrics communicate the sheer ecstasy of being in love, when the good, the pleasurable, mundane and ugly experiences are all powerless to induce an iota of negativity or affect the mood. This character is seeing sheer delight in everything and it's sparkling and infectious. This is the happiest song to this point in the discography, and probably its most contented and joyous piece, period.

'Love' (Joni Mitchell)

Released as a single B-side, November 1982 (US), 19 November 1982 (UK), December 1982 (CA), b/w '(You're So Square) Baby, I Don't Care'.

In 1982, Joni was involved in the short film anthology, *Love*. She worked on Swedish director Mai Zetterling's short, *Black Cat in the Black Mouse Socks*. But it was Norwegian director Liv Ullmann's short, *Parting*, that supplied the inspiration for this song. In the short, Charles Jolliffe played an elderly man who read the New Testament's *Corinthians I:13* to his bedridden wife. It was Jolliffe who at the movie's wrap party suggested to Joni she write a song based on the passage.

Adapting St. Paul's virtually 2000-year-old text required some restructuring. But Joni added only one word: 'fractions'. 'Fractions in me of faith and hope and love'. She felt the text summarised the entire subject. She has since claimed the song to be a perfect synopsis of every love song she ever wrote. Indeed the track had aspects of *Court and Spark* disposition and *Blue* soul-searching. And if it's divine presence you're after, try guitarist Steve Lukather's moving low-frequency chords swelling in intermittently from 2m:09s, for a real shiver down the spine.

Contemporary Tracks

'Why Do Fools Fall in Love? (Live)' (Frankie Lymon, Jimmy Merchant, Herman Santiago)

Released on the live album Shadows and Light (1980) and as a single A-side, August 1980 (US), 24 October 1980 (UK), October 1980 (CA), 27 October 1980 (AU), b/w 'Black Crow (Live)'. US: 102.

The early '80s '50s revival was by now in full mainstream swing thanks to smashes like Queen's 'Crazy Little Thing Called Love'. Predominantly-rockabilly singles kept coming via groups like Stray Cats. Doo-wop had its revival too with hits like the Manhattan Transfer's 1981 cover of The Adlibs' 1964 hit, 'The Boy From New York City'.

It's convenient that this single from Joni's second live album *Shadows and Light* – cut in September 1979 at the Santa Barbara Bowl – happened to slot into the trend. Without it, she may not have had a single at all in 1980, considering the live album was virtually wall-to-wall late-'70s hardcore album cuts. Taken slightly faster than Frankie Lymon & the Teenagers' 1956 original, this take was certainly authentic, helped largely by the presence of vocal group, The Persuasions. Otherwise, it consisted only of Don Alias on drums and the sublime tenor saxophone of Michael Brecker.

One year later, soul singer, Diana Ross' updated '60s-Motown-ified version, made the song a worldwide hit again. Joni's single may not have broken through, but it *was* her first US singles chart appearance in four years.

'Two Grey Rooms (Demo)' (Joni Mitchell)

Released in the box set Joni Mitchell: The Complete Geffen Recordings, 2003.

After a *Wild Things Run Fast* session at A&M one night, drummer, Vinnie Coliauta, keen to keep working, asked if Joni had anything else they could play. She did have an instrumental piano piece, but the instrument, reserved for a Michel Colombier session, displayed a do-not-touch sign. Joni convinced engineer Henry Lewy to open it up so she could play just this one take of the unfinished song. That night she sang two takes of a wordless vocal on it, naming the piece 'Speechless' until she had a lyric. That would eventuate in 1989 when the final vocal was recorded as 'Two Grey Rooms', and the track released on 1991's *Night Ride Home*.

Dog Eat Dog (1985)

Personnel:
Vocals, Piano, Keyboards, Vocal samples: Joni Mitchell
Backing vocals: Don Henley, Amy Holland, Michael McDonald, Joni Mitchell, James Taylor
Bass: Larry Klein
Bata: Alex Acuna
Drums, Samples: Vinnie Colaiuta
Evangelist speech: Rod Steiger ('Tax Free')
Flugelhorn, Trumpet: Gary Grant, Jerry Hey
Flute: Larry Williams
Guest vocal: Michael McDonald ('Good Friends')
Guitar: Michael Landau, Steve Lukather
Keyboards, Programming: Thomas Dolby, Larry Klein
Percussion samples: Michael Fisher
Shakuhachi: Kazu Matsui
Spoken vocals: Thomas Dolby, Larry Klein, Joe Smith, Bob 'Zyg' Winard
Saxophone: Wayne Shorter, Larry Williams
Recorded February-September 1985 at Galaxy Studios, Los Angeles, CA.
Producers: Thomas Dolby, Larry Klein, Joni Mitchell, Mike Shipley
Engineers: Mike Shipley, Bob 'Zyg' Winard, Dan Marnien
Arranger: Jerry Hey (Horns)
Label: Geffen
US Release date: October 1985. UK Release date: November 1985.
Chart placings: US: 63, UK: 57, CAN: 44, AU: 86, NZ: 30, SE: 27

The initial spark for the protest statement that was *Dog Eat Dog* came in 1983. Joni was one of twelve artists (Neil Young and America among them) in California who had 85 per cent of their income from 1971 to 1977 rescinded through an arbitrary wholesale tax. Enraged, this reawakened her politically, the event's inequity coming to the forefront of her music.

Formerly she hadn't considered politics to be the musician's business. Now she thought it was everyone's business. She had become all too aware of 'The crookedness of government and the power struggle going on in America'. She battled the State of California for ten years and finally won. Her housekeeper suing her for $5,000,000 further propelled the already blazing inferno. That laughable case was thrown out of court.

Otherwise, post the 1983 World Tour, married life was idyllic. 1984 was spent at home watching a lot of TV, writing and recording eight-track demos with Larry Klein for the album that would be fuelled by the new political convictions. Slightly more well-equipped than your average 1984 home demo setup, theirs consisted of the standard drum-machine-and-a-couple-of-keyboards, plus £30,000 worth of Series II Fairlight CMI sampling technology. They were keen to assimilate the new sounds into the work – Larry even getting up early to take Fairlight lessons. The new machinery inspired Joni. 'All the sampling, the use of found sounds – these are ideas I started working with back in the '70s. But there was no climate for them then and I was ridiculed, in a way. Now it's all open, so exciting. It makes me want to get back on that track and do some things I was kind of shocked out of.'.

On Sunday 10 February 1985, Joni joined multiple Canadian pop singers in Vancouver to record the famine relief single 'Tears Are Not Enough' under the artist name Northern Lights. This was two months after the release of Band Aid's 'Feed the World' in the UK, and three weeks after the recording of USA For Africa's 'We Are the World' but a month before its release. After the interlude – which included fellow Canadians Bryan Adams, Neil Young and Rush's Geddy Lee – it was back to L.A. to record *Dog Eat Dog*.

Sessions took place mostly at night, with Klein working afternoons on Wayne Shorter's first solo album since 1974, *Atlantis*. Using the technology, Joni and Larry still wanted spontaneity on the sessions and felt they needed someone to handle the equipment's complex functions. Enter Australian engineer/producer, Mike Shipley. Joni had been advised to use a producer on the project. Geffen Records had offered the gig to British synthesizer wiz, Thomas Dolby. Chic guitarist and current hot producer, Nile Rodgers, was also a name in the hat. But to Joni, the thought of any producer was painful. That was generally 'A guy that watches football games on the studio TV, talks on the phone and throws his weight around'. But the need for an extra person led to calling Dolby with an offer to function as player and Fairlight programmer, which he accepted. Joni knew Dolby had good intentions, but with him being used to being a front-liner, she had her doubts whether he would be happy coming in as a virtual foot soldier and subordinating his ideas. In discussion, he said, 'I would love to do it. I am sick of people always looking to me for the answer'. In the end, it was a co-production between all four, minus a Dolby credit on 'The Three Great Stimulants' and 'Ethiopia'. 'Smokin' (Empty, Try Another)', produced by Joni, was a leftover from the *Wild Things Run Fast* sessions.

A microphone just happened to be recording as Dolby arrived for his first day at the studio. His lethargic comment 'Oh I'm so excited' tickled Joni pink to the point where it was eventually sampled and included in 'Shiny Toys'. But the association had its strains. Dolby would build up piles of instrument tracks and Joni would have to remind him he was hired primarily for his Fairlight expertise. Wrong or right, she couldn't give over that much territory, so those tracks were never used. She told *New Musical Express* in 1985, 'I don't want to be interior-decorated out of my own music. He may be able to do it faster. He may even be able to do it better, but the fact is it won't really be my music.'. Further issues appeared when it came to vocal time. The pair would disagree on which lines were keepers. Management encouraging Dolby behind Joni's back – along with what I deduce from the literature to be the label telling each of them whatever was necessary to keep them together and leaving them to deal with the fallout – probably didn't help the situation for both of them. Ultimately, Joni loved the end result.

Coincidentally, during the making of *Dog Eat Dog*, Joni and long-time manager, Elliot Roberts, parted ways. Then initially managing herself, the reality was the phone never stopped ringing. So she hired old friend – and Linda Ronstadt and James Taylor manager – Peter Asher. Around this time, Joni was asked to appear on 'Sun City', an anti-apartheid record protesting performances at the internationally unrecognised South African resort of the same name. But she refused to participate upon discovering the initial lyric virtually pilloried acts who'd performed there, among them her good friend, Ronstadt, who'd innocently undertaken the gig from the standpoint that art should cross any border.

In August 1985, towards album completion, a drunk driver ploughed into Joni and Larry on the Pacific Coast Highway, totalling the car and causing Joni's head to shatter the windscreen. They walked away with barely a scratch.

Dog Eat Dog was the most expensive and difficult record Joni ever made. It was a different approach again. She was still exploring, telling one interviewer she felt like Paul Revere making the record. She'd always been a free agent, but the business had changed. There was a crack-down now. She had to fight to even get a gatefold cover, which were now reserved for only the largest profit-makers. Music itself had made an about-turn. In the '70s, musicians had been more orthodox and radio more liberal. By 1985 it was the other way around. Where the press once criticised Joni for crossing over into jazz, now an artist like Sting was perceived as blazing a trail doing exactly the same thing. 'One year you're persecuted for it, the next you're hip because of it'. Joni thought this change might benefit *Dog Eat Dog.* But despite Wayne Shorter's sax solos, it wasn't particularly anchored in jazz style with the exception perhaps of 'Lucky Girl'. She knew one thing for sure – 'If a corporation can make a profit on what you do, they'll leave you alone. If this does well, I can afford to do it again next year. If it doesn't, it'll be back to Joni and her guitar'.

The timing was right. In September 1985, rock star, Prince, broke his silence with an extended interview in *Rolling Stone* where he praised Joni's album, *The Hissing of Summer Lawns*. Sales of that record subsequently went through the roof, Joni realising how much weight the endorsement of those currently in vogue carried.

On Monday 28 October, Geffen Records threw a *Dog Eat Dog* release party at the James Corcoran Gallery in Santa Monica, L.A. The event, a Museum of Contemporary Art benefit, also displayed Joni's paintings.

Sadly, the album's cutting-edge sound didn't preclude some press criticism of its politics. *Time* magazine described some of the subject matter as adolescent. Joni ahead of the times, again – two of the songs covered topics that *Time* themselves would feature as cover stories soon enough.

The cover painting, perhaps her most provocative yet, showed her howling in defiance of the predators surrounding her. That said it all. But it wasn't everything. As she told Terry Wogan on the *Wogan* show in London in December, 'the album starts with a song about friends and ends with a song about love, with some other stuff in the middle.' He then asked what she attributed her longevity in the business to. She replied, 'Smoking and drinking.'.

'Good Friends' (Joni Mitchell)

Released as a single A-side, November 1985 (US), 18 November 1985 (UK), b/w 'Smokin' (Empty, Try Another)'. US: 85.
Released as a 12" and CD single B-side, 1988 (UK and DE), b/w 'My Secret Place', 'Number One' and 'Chinese Cafe/Unchained Melody'.

Things had changed since the days of 'Big Yellow Taxi', when aesthetics were more considered, and a key single could be safely placed towards the end of an album. Now the thing was to put it as the opener as if money was the primary concern, which for a label it certainly was. The duet with Doobie Brothers vocalist/keyboardist, Michael McDonald, *was* the obvious starter though. Joni knew all along that his was the voice to play the other character. Promotional effort was put behind the record, including an animated music video by Jim Blashfield. On Friday 6 December 1985, Joni sang the song live to a backing track and a studio audience on the *Wogan* TV show in London. Standing in for Michael McDonald was Modern Romance singer, Michael J. Mullins, who did a fine job with such shoes to fill. But neither that awkward visual nor the official video garnered the song a UK singles chart appearance – the lyric's intellectual friendship analysis requiring perhaps too much effort on a listener's part.

Nevertheless, the poppy-sounding uptempo track was worthy of Joni's finest work. Technology was to the forefront from the first measure. Drums were programmed and samples (vocal) were used for the first time since she'd practically experimented with the as-yet-unnamed technique on 1975's 'The Jungle Line'. The 'Good Friends' 'see' and 'you' intro vocal harmony repeats were recorded separately and triggered back in as a digital delay. Mike Landau's whammy-bar rhythm guitar throughout was also a sonic highlight.

The basic lyric outline of a non-judgmental friendship was twisted into irony in verse three where suddenly the two characters bickered.

But now it's cloak and dagger
Walk on eggshells and analyse
Every particle of difference
Gets like mountains in our eyes
You say "You're unscrupulous!"
You say "You're naive!"
Synchronised like magic
Good friends you and me

The 1984 demo was included in the 2003 box set, *Joni Mitchell: The Complete Geffen Recordings*.

'Fiction' (Joni Mitchell, Larry Klein)

Written by Larry Klein, this music required lyrics to be placed on short melodic phrases. Joni was used to lengthy line metrics, so it was a challenge. Finding the words 'truth' and 'fiction' gave a clear direction, to the point where there were pages of lyrics. 'Fiction' expanded on the consumerism idea first hinted at in the 'Sweet Bird' line, 'All these vain promises on beauty jars'. The momentary sampled voices of Klein, Thomas Dolby and Joe Smith in sell-mode, anticipated 1988's 'The Reoccurring Dream', a song which took the technique to an extreme. But 'Fiction' expanded the consumer concept further into one of conspiracy, progressing (regressing?) into cynicism and a general lack of faith leading to frustration.

> Fiction of declaimers
> Fiction of rebukers
> Fiction of the pro and the no-nukers
> Fiction of the gizmo
> Fiction of the data
> Fiction of this is this and that is that ahh!

As relevant now as it was then. Probably more. And it was all atop the catchiest – if oblique – robotic programmed drum rhythm 1985 could muster. The politics of dancing, indeed.

'The Three Great Stimulants' (Joni Mitchell)

Released as a single B-side, April 1986 (UK), May 1986 (US), b/w 'Shiny Toys'. Released as a 12" single B-side, 1986 (UK and France), b/w 'Shiny Toys (Extended remix)' and 'Ethiopia'.

Guitar was the initial home for this rhythmically broken-down sociological-statement ballad. But when transposed up a fourth and keyboard-dominated, it became more a presentation of the available technology. But the lyric concept was equally, if not more, substantial. It borrowed from the German philosopher Nietzsche's 1899 essay on German composer, Wagner.

> Wagner is the modern artist par excellence, the Cagliostro of modernism. In his art there is mixed, in the most seductive manner, the things at present most necessary for everybody, the three great stimulants of the exhausted, brutality, artifice, and innocence (idiocy).

By 1985, little had changed. In interviews at the time, Joni pointed out that whenever she wore flamboyant make-up, she couldn't keep people away. They were responding to what she called the seduction of artifice. Brutality too was big business if, for example, the success of slasher movies was anything to go by. As for innocence, she claimed that a country entering into decadence spawns an envy of youth. In the '80s, thousands of ageing hippies enduring constant gym torture was a testament to this; lack of experience was refreshing, and the need to be young, appealing.

Sound effects reflected the lyric's foreboding elements. First laid-down was the rhythmic helicopter 'fit-fit-fit' – a sound then still highly evocative ten years after the close of the Vietnam War. A Super-8 movie Joni had made of some wall graffiti in Soho, Manhattan, yielded a builder hammering over a blaring burglar alarm. This was sampled and used in the bridge sections, audible in its natural ambience on the left side for six bars after the words 'Deep in the night'. Everyone but Joni thought the sample lacked adequate fidelity. But she knew it would lose its essence through a recreation, so it was kept.

Musical counterparts represented the three elements of artifice, brutality and innocence. For the latter, a synthesizer harp sound played a simple chorus figure. No one there but Joni liked *that* sound either. I guessed it to be a Dolby timbre, the likes of which you'd hear on his Prefab Sprout productions ongoing. It appeared to me that once Dolby found a sound he liked, he often used it for years.

Back to the three elements. From the second chorus on, at the word 'brutality', a fierce guitar slide panned across the soundstage to a barely audible percussive strike from Stravinsky's 'The Rite of Spring'. 'Artifice' came via the slightly louder sample of pop singer Madonna's exclamation of 'Hey!' from the chorus of 'Like a Virgin'. If you're familiar with 'The Three Great Stimulants' and you've never noticed that particular detail before, take warning – once heard, you can't unhear it. These were all welcome cultural touches, however subtle. At a time when samples were generally prominent and overused to gimmick effect, their indirect use here was an eccentric detail, left as textural and complementary.

'Tax Free' (Joni Mitchell, Larry Klein)

1985 was the beginning of the PMRC (Parents Music Resource Center) and their attack on the music industry through the introduction of legislation enforcing album cover warning stickers. 'Tax Free' protested both music censorship and self-righteous moral-majority evangelism. The irony was that the latter filled the same stadiums as the rock shows, therefore existing on an equal footing – that is, as show business. Joni felt it appropriate to speak up in song.

God's hired hands and the devil bands
Packing the same grandstands

You get witch-hunts and wars
When church and state hold hands

American actor, Rod Steiger, was the ideal choice to execute the song's focal-point intermittent preaching howl. In 1979, he'd done at least as much in the best scene of the otherwise questionable but popular horror movie, *The Amityville Horror*. He also was no stranger to controversy after starring in 1964's *The Pawnbroker.* Moving Steiger to the upper echelon of actors, that movie drew much additional attention by being among the first to have a defined gay character and nudity that passed (what was then known as) the Production Code standard. By decade's end, the code had collapsed and been restructured into the Motion Picture Association film rating system. So when Joni and Larry met their close neighbour, Steiger, at the local drugstore, played him the tape and asked him to recite on the recording, the answer was yes.

Steiger's raving evangelist monologue was broken up throughout the track. But the ironic anti-evangelism message it touted was clear. 'Multiple hundreds of thousands of hundreds and millions of dollars. A hundred billion dollars! And who is paying the price? Your children are.'

The retaliatory lyrics set Larry Klein's beautiful chord progression alight. As with the album's other Klein collaboration, 'Fiction', placing lyrics on the fragmentary melodic lines proved to be a challenge. But it worked, as if the stunted bi-syllabic exclamations mirrored the inherent frustration. 'Cheap talk, Deep talk', 'Jacked up'. In verse two, the combined forces of backing singers Don Henley, Michael McDonald, James Taylor and recent pop success Amy Holland, drove a spike of their own into the target, through a partial quote of the hymn, 'O Come All Ye Faithful'. The lyric line was twisted up to come from the target's mouth as, 'Oh come let us adore – ME!'.

'Smokin' (Empty, Try Another)' (Joni Mitchell)

Released as a single B-side, November 1985 (US), 18 November 1985 (UK), b/w 'Good Friends'.

The parking lot cigarette machine at A&M Studios was not well-maintained. Running out of cigarette packs, it would regularly display the lit message 'Empty, try another' as the gears made a rhythmic pattern of movement and squeaks with a natural backbeat. Bogged down one evening during the recording of *Wild Things Run Fast*, Joni needed an idea to get things moving. Then she had the eureka moment. They ran an extension cord outside, placed a microphone inside the cigarette machine, and recorded four minutes of the cycle.

Armed with the recording, everyone else wanted to sample it, but Joni felt it sounded perfect as is. Like the hammer and burglar alarm sample in 'The Three Great Stimulants', she saw no sense in changing the sound's natural character.

After adding Larry Klein's improvised fretless bass lines and Steve Lukather's liquid guitar punctuations, Joni sang a chant, solo and in block harmony. Not fitting the romantic mood of *Wild Things Run Fast*, the avant-garde piece was resurrected for *Dog Eat Dog*, where it contrasted well against the 'Fiction' consumerism theme.

'Dog Eat Dog' (Joni Mitchell)

The title track spoke plainly of waking up to the decline of western culture. Don Henley and James Taylor joined in on backing vocals, in support of both song and notion I'm sure. The musical arrangement was kept reserved, ensuring a clear message. It was indeed an acoustic piano song to begin with, as performed solo, live on London's Capitol Radio in December 1985. But even the modest album version – taken at a medium tempo in the broken-down rhythm fashion of the day – couldn't hide the continued willingness to explore and push boundaries. The lyric line lengths varied, stopping and starting as if in a panic about the situation. The lines, 'Holy hope in the hands of snakebite evangelists and racketeers, and big wig financiers', were so obliquely placed that you barely even noticed the rhyme.

Still generally relevant today, one stanza even appeared to predict the 21st century.

> Land of snap decisions
> Land of short attention spans
> Nothing is savoured long enough to really understand

'Shiny Toys' (Joni Mitchell)

Released as a 7" single A-side, April 1986 (UK), May 1986 (US), b/w 'The Three Great Stimulants'.
Released as a 12" single A-side Extended Remix, 1986 (UK and France), b/w 'Ethiopia' and 'The Three Great Stimulants'.

The second single continued on a topical theme but from the spectrum's lighter end. The focus was on the joys of having money, with a subtext of it being the root of all evil. Joni told an interviewer at the time that she liked money itself but not what it did to people. She claimed she could live with much less, that it's better to have nothing, and even that artists should be kept starving as it keeps them honest, resurrecting ideas expounded upon in 1975's 'The Boho Dance'.

But these ideas weren't obvious from the track's uptempo and joyous sound. The music video too, shot in black and white, was a simple celebration of happiness, showing Joni dancing alfresco, with and without guitar. Humour made an appearance when after the line, 'What ever makes your time feel satisfying', Joni lip-synced to the sample of Thomas Dolby arriving at the studio saying, 'Oh I'm so excited'. 'I love Miss September' with the following single sentence. 'The Francis Kevorkian 12'' extended mix had additional voiceovers, including Bob 'Zyg' Winard's statement of 'I love my Porsche' and Thomas Dolby's 'I love Miss September'. Towards the end is a synthesizer solo on a woody flute patch, presumably played by Dolby, although it shows nothing particularly characteristic to suggest it was him.

In general, the album cut featured a contemporary arrangement style, certainly on the choruses where every instrumental figure had its defined place in time and nothing tread on any other toes. Backing vocals came again from Don Henley and James Taylor. But the cherry on top was Jerry Hey's horn arrangement – a combination of chord stabs (Some from a sampler I'm certain) and a patently '60s Burt Bacharach touch.

'Ethiopia' (Joni Mitchell)

Released as a 12" single B-side, 1986 (UK and France), b/w 'Shiny Toys (Extended remix)' and 'The Three Great Stimulants'.

After participating in the Canadian famine relief record 'Tears Are Not Enough' in February 1985, Joni wrote the more caustic, atmospheric ballad, 'Ethiopia'. Several problems frustrated her; The West's attitude towards African famine as a removed Third World problem without realising it as a global ecology crisis; The general self-congratulatory overtone of famine relief records like 'We Are the World' (which she felt could be narrowed down simply to 'We'); And the sheer expense of presenting these live and recorded events, which, along with governments at both ends, plundered the money that failed to filter through to the intended recipients. Her key phrase to interviewers was, 'There's the appearance of wheels in motion and then there's the actual motion.'. A case in point was the first-ever large-scale benefit concert, 1971's *Concert for Bangladesh.* Despite organiser George Harrison's efforts, funds raised were tied up in escrow until 1984. A similar fate befell 1979's *No Nukes* concert funds. It was too soon to tell in the case of July 1985's Live Aid concert.

Specific lyrics protested these very ideas; 'On and on insanities, On and on short-sighted greed abounds'. Other lines spoke in more general ecological terms; 'Your topsoil flies away, We pump ours full of poison spray'. Beneath the chorus hook lay a tribal percussion sample, updating the tape loop technique used on 1975's 'The Jungle Line'.

'Ethiopia' was the album's most poignant tribute. And as much as its music was exquisite and alluring, Joni likely would've preferred she'd never had to write it.

'Impossible Dreamer' (Joni Mitchell)

The single potential here was obvious. Despite the negative title, the track was gleaming and the choruses upbeat. The political climate had reignited in some the ideals of Martin Luther King and John Lennon, who were among people Joni called the impossible dreamers. She told *Melody Maker* in 1986, 'It's kind of a tip of the hat to the beautiful idealists that, ironically, most of them were assassinated. Almost like the very presence of that idealism drew down immense hostility. With a few rare exceptions, this is not a heart time. Anything with that kind of delicacy is fair game in a way. It's a fun time, let's have fun.'.

Where the lyric's 'blue shadows' were perhaps one metaphor for the lost ideals, Wayne Shorter's soprano saxophone lines certainly stood in support of the daylight that illuminated the chorus, one of Joni's most graceful.

In the darkest part of the night
Blue shadows conjure you
And in the brightest height of the daylight
Sometimes I blink 'cause I think I see you
Dreaming like you do

By default, 'Impossible Dreamer' appeared to be the closest Joni came to contributing to the stream of John Lennon tributes that were still coming in 1985. He had after all so publicly perceived himself as being judged as a dreamer. Perhaps Ludwig Van Beethoven was also one of those impossible dreamers. The introduction's upper chord melody voice was almost identical to that of the *For the Roses* Beethoven tribute, 'Judgement of the Moon and Stars'.

'Lucky Girl' (Joni Mitchell)

After all the criticism received for previously heading in a jazz direction, Joni was bewildered when at a *Dog Eat Dog* playback, a label executive exclaimed, 'Oh I really really like this one. It's jazzy!'. Joni thought she'd die. The label even considered 'Lucky Girl' as a single. As if out of nowhere, jazz was suddenly hip again, thanks largely to the huge influence of British rock star, Sting, and his personal quest to bring more jazz virtuosity to pop music. This he'd certainly achieved with his then-current solo debut, the hugely successful *The Dream of the Blue Turtles*, where he was flanked by a battery of jazz talent. If the pop business could simply turn on a dime like that, it made all of Joni's genre-related pain and suffering a complete waste of time. It certainly spoke nothing of her music's merit at any point in the timeline. If the *Mingus* album had come out in 1985, 'The Dry Cleaner from Des Moines' would've had every chance at becoming a hit. But, the world isn't fair.

It probably didn't matter much now. 'Lucky Girl' was an unashamedly positive declaration of Joni's love for her husband, Klein. 'I never loved a man I trusted, As far as I could pitch my shoe, 'Til I loved you'. She even described the song as the album's happy Hollywood ending.

Contemporary Tracks

'Good Friends (Demo)' (Joni Mitchell)

Released in the box set Joni Mitchell: The Complete Geffen Recordings, 2003.

Minus this track's flashy electronic costume, the 1984 solo piano demo is a good window into the song's inherent substance.

Chalk Mark in a Rain Storm (1988)

Personnel:
Vocals, Drum programming, Guitar, Keyboards: Joni Mitchell
Bass: Larry Klein
Backing Vocals: Lisa Coleman, Don Henley, Manu Katche, Larry Klein, Michael Landau, Julie Last, Wendy Melvoin, Joni Mitchell, Benjamin Orr
Collage: Joni Mitchell ('The Reoccurring Dream')
Drums: Manu Katche
Drum programming: Joni Mitchell
Fairlight marimba: Thomas Dolby
Guest vocalists: Iron Eyes Cody, Peter Gabriel, Don Henley, Billy Idol, Willie Nelson, Tom Petty
Guitar: Michael Landau, Steve Stevens
Keyboards: Larry Klein
Organ: Steve Lindsey
Percussion: Manu Katche
Saxophone: Wayne Shorter
Recorded 1986-1987 at Ashcombe House, Bath, UK; The Wool Hall, Beckington, UK; Artisan Recording Studios, A&M Studios, Galaxy Studios, Ocean Way, Sound Castle and Village Recorders, Los Angeles, CA; Ground Control, Santa Monica, CA.
Producers: Joni Mitchell, Larry Klein
Engineers: David Botteril, Richard Cottrell, Angus Davidson, Chris Fuhrman, Fred Howard, Bill Jenkins, Robin Lane, Julie Last, Henry Lewy, Dan Marnien, Rick O'Neil, John Payne, Mike Ross, Mike Shipley, Alan Smart, Dave Stallbaumer
Label: Geffen
US Release date: 23 March 1988. UK Release date: March 1988.
Chart placings: US: 45, UK: 26, CAN: 23, AU: 44, NZ: 18, SE: 37.

Where *Dog Eat Dog* had been a kind of rage against the political machine, *Chalk Mark in a Rain Storm* was a necessary come down in order to rise above the angst. This time Larry Klein prevented tracks becoming wild and overgrown, allowing the songs to breathe more freely. In a way, it was Joni's job to plant and Larry's job to prune. Joni later explained her mindset moving through that phase.

> Wherever there was a hollow I'd put a musical figure in it that had two hollows in it like a W. In those two hollows I'd plant another figure with a hollow in it and then put the cherry on the pudding.

Considering its tamer, more organic production, *Chalk Mark* was still a colourful beast and its large cast of characters led Joni to allude to it as a rock opera with no storyline.

The record began life in England in early 1986. Larry Klein had travelled to the Wool Hall at Beckington to produce an album for The Cars' bassist/vocalist

Ben Orr. Hearing Larry was in the area, Peter Gabriel invited him out to his personal studio at Ashcombe House near Bath to play on his virtually complete album, *So*. Joni had two new songs ready, and with Gabriel's studio now free, he suggested she record there as his guest. Co-opting Gabriel's drummer, Manu Katche, they launched into 'My Secret Place', Joni putting Gabriel to work as the duet's male half.

At the time, the world was in political turmoil. First, US forces launched part of the Libya bombing raid from an airfield across the valley from Ashcombe House. Then within weeks, there was fear from the radioactive cloud floating across Northern Europe as a result of the Chernobyl disaster. This all contributed to the creation of the war-themed 'The Beat of Black Wings', a theme that also existed around the periphery of 'The Tea Leaf Prophecy'.

Back in the USA, Joni continued with the novelty of inviting vocalists to appear on the songs. Willie Nelson came in to sing on 'Cool Water', and Billy Idol and Tom Petty were enlisted as the male characters on 'Dancin' Clown'. The Eagles' Don Henley played the male in the effective duet 'Snakes and Ladders'.

Prince & the Revolution members, Wendy Melvoin and Lisa Coleman, sang backing vocals on 'The Tea Leaf Prophecy'. Joni met them through Prince, who'd begun inviting her to various events. She even appeared onstage for the Revolution's second encore at Denver's McNichols Arena on Friday 3 July 1987. But Wendy and Lisa's appearance on the track eventuated through the tried-and-true method of bumping into them at the studio. Around this period there were rumours of a Joni and Prince collaboration. He had suggested that Joni's open harmony over his funk could make an interesting hybrid. In 1994 she confirmed that he once sent her just one song, titled 'Emotional Pump'. But work on it never eventuated. Now available on the 2020 *Sign o' the Times* deluxe edition, the track appears to me to have shown little opportunity for logical Joni inclusion.

In the summer of 1987, Joni was also unable to connect any longer with her treasured Mercedes Benz – nicknamed Bluebird – which she'd bought in 1969 with her first royalty cheque. One warm night she stopped into Tower Records on Sunset Blvd, craving hearing the Jimmy Cliff record, 'Bongo Man'. Stepping back outside, the beloved car had disappeared.

Much worse was the tragic death of bassist, Jaco Pastorius, on Monday 21 September – truly the end of an era in more ways than one. Joni credited his influence with causing her to hear music in a way she never had before the two met.

More happily, Joni and Larry's home studio – a bedroom conversion which would be known as The Kiva – was begun in early 1988 and wired-up in May. But before that could be utilised, there was the *Chalk Mark* release fallout to manoeuvre (fingers crossed), and a year of promotional touring to undergo. Joni found the press reaction to the album baffling. They'd disliked *Dog Eat Dog* but loved *Chalk Mark*. She saw no real difference, considering the latter an extension of the former. But she was pleased. The last two albums had been expensive to make and there was still the real necessity to break even. 'You can be doing great work, but unless people buy it, you're condemned to obscurity and it's only a matter of time before that's it for you'.

The album's relative success was a triumph after years lacking real record company support. And of all the reviews, it was Janet Jackson's endorsement ten years later that meant the most. Being interviewed for her then-current album *The Velvet Rope*, she played Joni's 'The Beat of Black Wings', saying, 'Never mind my album. Listen to *this*. This is on a whole other level.'.

Despite the pensive album cover photo-portrait (Courtesy of Larry Klein), times were good. The shot was clearly taken on the 'My Secret Place' video shoot – a video brimming over with good humour.

'My Secret Place' (Joni Mitchell)

Released as a 7" single A-side (Edit), May 1988 (UK and AU), b/w 'Number One'.
Released as a 7" single A-side (Album version), 1988 (DE), b/w 'Number One'.
Released as a 7" single A-side (Edit), June 1988 (CA), July 1988 (US), 1988 (DE), b/w 'Lakota'. CA: 44.
Released as a 12" and CD single A-side, 1988 (UK and DE), b/w 'Number One', 'Chinese Cafe/Unchained Melody' and 'Good Friends'.

The first single was recorded in April 1986, two years prior to the album release, and was among the last tracks recorded at Peter Gabriel's home of Ashcombe House in Somerset, England. I've always heard 'My Secret Place' as an unlikely album opener – a bit laid back, even standoff-ish. For me, 'Lakota' was the track that had that introductory flavour, with the tension that builds towards that first album vocal. But 'My Secret Place' happened to be the single and made for a more positive album launching pad. It represented the beginning threshold and double-minded optimism of a new relationship, where nothing is held back. Guitars certainly weren't held back, with 20 tracks of Martin acoustic employed to achieve that thick warm resonance.

To further delineate the concept, the lead vocals – a duet between Joni and Peter Gabriel – were mixed to appropriate the oneness of a spiritual union. The changes between voices were almost unnoticeable – halfway through lines and sometimes in the middle of a word – the ideas more communal, as opposed to one person speaking to the other.

Lyrically, the male whisked the female New Yorker off to his Colorado hideaway. A sense of humour was present throughout director Anton Corbijn's black and white music video art piece. Mitchell and Gabriel faced each other at the dinner table, the track vocals their conversation, looking as if they'd both explode with laughter any second. Joni's outdoor-shot voice-over, 'There's a place I know that I'd really like to take you to.', was a tasteful non-album overdub. The video also utilised the full album-length version and not the 3m:17s single edit issued in some territories.

'Number One' (Joni Mitchell)

Released as a single B-side, May 1988 (UK and AU), b/w 'My Secret Place'.
Released as a single B-side, 1988 (DE), b/w 'My Secret Place (Album version)'.
Released as a 12" and CD single B-side, 1988 (UK and DE), b/w 'My Secret Place', 'Chinese Cafe/Unchained Melody' and 'Good Friends'.

Recording in England in 1986, Joni and Larry met with Led Zeppelin singer Robert Plant. Then in between projects, he was looking for songs with a view to completing something unfinished of Larry's. Joni sat down with a guitar and sang 'My Secret Place' and 'Number One'. Plant was reverent. After she left the room, he said to Larry, 'Tell her that a man should sing that second song'. The song's forthright take on ambition would've worked well for Plant's then-current approach. He wanted the song but didn't get it. Joni identified closely with its contrary indifference. She even performed it for an antagonistic audience at the *Conspiracy of Hope* Amnesty International benefit concert – where she filled in for Pete Townshend – on Sunday 15 June 1986 at Giants Stadium in East Rutherford, New Jersey. She felt the irony was perfect – 'Will they shower you with flowers, or will they shun ya, when your race is run?'. As the album recording progressed, she also finagled two instrumentals Larry wrote specifically for Plant – 'Lakota' and 'Snakes and Ladders'. In the end, Plant, in good humour, made the request, 'Would you please stop nicking my songs?'.

The track's characteristic programmed drum pattern got its swing from sampling the multi-track tape flipping when wound to the end of a reel, and inserting it in the track to sound like an open hi-hat. This was the first such structural programming to occur on this album, though it would generally absorb such elements to comfortably co-exist with the organic instrumentation.

'Lakota' (Joni Mitchell, Larry Klein)

Released as a single B-side, June 1988 (CA), July 1988 (US), 1988 (DE), b/w 'My Secret Place (Edit)'.

Larry Klein first cut this instrumental track with a view to Robert Plant writing a song over it. But when Joni heard it, she heard a potential anthem for the American Indian in its often static chord movement. Part-American-Indian herself, she felt a particular affinity with their concerns. Having sung it (with the help of The Eagles' Don Henley on backing vocals), all she needed was approval that the chants had an authenticity.

Temporarily unable to record due to a studio hardware issue, Joni used an evening to attend a pow wow held at the Santa Monica Civic Arena. There she met American actor, Iron Eyes Cody, and brought him back to the studio, where he then sang the solo introductory chant. After his departure, Joni realised that in her enthusiasm she'd forgotten to check if he was in tune with the track. Luckily he was and part of his chant was sampled and placed throughout the song.

The album's primary political vehicle, 'Lakota' addressed the plight of the Lakota nation and their uneasy relationship with the US government over its coveting of their uranium-rich land. The song had a positive effect. The chief of the Lakota Sioux heard it and invited Joni and Iron Eyes Cody to appear as dignitaries on a protest march scheduled for 16 March 1988. It was there that Joni shot the Super-8 footage used for the music video. Royalties generated by the song went to charity.

'The Tea Leaf Prophecy (Lay Down Your Arms)' (Joni Mitchell, Larry Klein)

Song four began life as another Larry Klein backing track looking for a lyric. It was based loosely on Joni's parents' World War II courtship in Regina, Saskatchewan. Thoughts of war were also prevalent in April 1986. The US strike force took off for Libya from several UK Air Force bases, including RAF Fairford, 40 miles adjacent to Joni stationed at Peter Gabriel's Bath studio, from where they saw the aircraft lights. This caused Joni to consider her father's time in the service and wartime turning points such as the 1945 nuclear bombings of Hiroshima and Nagasaki.

Lyrically, artistic license played a part with Joni changing her mother's name from Myrtle to Molly. But biography predominated with the included details of her parents' blind date leading to their marriage within a month (and Joni's birth within the year.). And it had all been predicted by a gipsy Myrtle visited, to whom she'd said, 'This is ridiculous. Look at this town. There's no men left, just frail old boys and babies'.

The backing vocals of Prince & the Revolution members, Wendy Melvoin and Lisa Coleman, came about in typical Joni fashion – bumping into them at the studio coffee machine and, of course, putting them to work.

It's worth quoting the last verse in its entirety as it's a poignant insight into Joni's understanding of a period of her infancy.

Sleep little darlin'
This is your happy home
Hiroshima cannot be pardoned!
Don't have kids when you get grown
Because this world is shattered
The wise are mourning
The fools are joking
Oh what does it matter?
The wash needs ironing
And the fire needs stoking

'Dancin' Clown' (Joni Mitchell)

Released as a CD single, 1988.

Having been told by the caretaker of her Canadian home that her songs were melancholy because she wrote them alone at night, Joni purposefully wrote 'Dancin' Clown' out in the sun. The song's character names, Rowdy Yates, Jesse and Suzie, all came from racehorses on a program from California's Santa Anita racetrack. Joni had no idea Rowdy Yates was Clint Eastwood's character from the American '60s western TV series, *Rawhide*.

The two male characters standing on a corner, watch the girl, Suzie, walk by. The brash Rowdy and the thin-skinned Jesse needed male singers to act their parts. Guest singers usually appeared through being in the vicinity of Joni recording, but this time she sought them out. She invited Billy Idol to record after seeing him at the 1987 Grammy Awards on Tuesday 24 February. The next night, he came by the studio and sang his part. Hearing the track, he insisted on calling in his guitar player, Steve Stevens, who obliged with his then in-demand signature power chords. If Stevens was given any freedom at all to solo, only one short, tasty line (At 2m:10s) survived the cut, though some bare gaps remained that could've utilised more. Mike Landau's comparatively liquid rhythm guitar part was clearly audible throughout.

The role of Jesse was first offered to Bob Dylan, who was willing, but conflicting schedules prevented it from happening. Tom Petty was then asked, and accepted, his character-wail proving perfect for the part.

The track's absolutely straight-four rhythm was likely the simplest ever heard on a Joni record. Bassist Klein played it completely straight, only allowing one string pop along the way. Drummer Manu Katche kept it as interesting as possible with a semi-broken-down but repetitive built-in tom figure. Thomas Dolby supplied a marimba synth part – his only contribution to the album – suggesting work on the backing track possibly began back in the *Dog Eat Dog* sessions, but this is pure speculation.

The song and its homemade music video were unpopular with some fans. The single failed to chart, and details of its existence are difficult to trace, despite my memory of regular airplay at the time. Prince, however, approved. He called Joni asking who it was hollering all over the track. When she said it was Billy Idol, he replied, 'That's a good idea'.

'Cool Water' (Joni Mitchell, Bob Nolan)

Released as a CD single (Edit), 1988 (US).

Don Henley had asked Joni to participate in a water issues benefit. Trying to come up with a new song for it, she suddenly remembered 'Cool Water'. The song by Canadian, Bob Nolan, had begun life as a poem which he added music to later. Joni slightly revised the lyrics – 'Some Devil's had a plan, buried poison in the sand'. But generally, any altered phrases retained their meaning in that charming manner that many old folk and country songs seem to naturally suffer over the years as if left out to the elements.

Country singer, Willie Nelson, pulled up to the studio in his Winnebago at 2:00 am after his nearby concert – most likely that in Riverside, CA, on Wednesday night 18 March 1987. Then and there, he sang on Joni's rendition of the 1936 country standard. She was in what she called 'heart mode', and therefore unable to guide Nelson through any possible weak performance aspects, considering she felt he was so gracious to come over in the middle of the night anyway. Larry pushed her, 'Joan, you know it's not quite right. Ask him to do it again'. It was an intellectual place she didn't particularly enjoy occupying, always preferring to give performers their freedom and digitally edit details into place herself afterwards. But Willie was as cooperative as could be.

Larry Klein programmed the introductory synthesizer sound from scratch. Joni called it 'Presbyterian in Peru' due to its South American flute character in the high notes and Gregorian-like choral in the low. Its atmosphere acted as a kind of sonic stepping stone towards the nocturnal ambience that was to colour *Night Ride Home*. Allof the above characteristics, combined with the luscious dissonance of guitarist Mike Landau's seductive chord work, gave *Chalk Mark* perhaps its most endearing passage.

'The Beat of Black Wings' (Joni Mitchell)

Peter Gabriel's home studio being so close to one of the bases from which U.S. planes attacked Libya in April 1986, combined with the Chernobyl disaster within two weeks, turned everyone's thoughts to war and how small the planet really was. That it got into the songwriting was inevitable. But the star of this lyric was Killer Kyle – the Vietnam paratrooper Joni had met in the late '60s and first mentioned in 1968's 'Cactus Tree'. This time the lyric told his horrific story replete with psychological fallout. 'The old hate the young, that's the whole heartless thing / The old pick the wars, we die in 'em'. His conclusion; 'I'm just a chalk mark in a rainstorm'.

Hearing Cars bassist Ben Orr's lower vocal register when he recorded with Larry, Joni thought Orr would be perfect for her place-keeper vocal percussion part intended for a talking drum. In the end, he sung the part over at Gabriel's studio, Joni's part was kept, and both were used in the final mix – a mix that wholeheartedly echoed the song's ticking-time-bomb psychology. But just as there's no dark without light, some relief appeared with each refrain's nostalgic recall of the 1962 Shelley Fabares number one, 'Johnny Angel'.

'Snakes and Ladders' (Joni Mitchell, Larry Klein)

Released as a promo single A-side and B-side, 1988 (US), b/w 'Snakes and Ladders'.

The album's other big love song after 'My Secret Place', was a kind of corporate love song. I don't mean as in record label single fodder (though it *was* sent to radio prior to album release), but corporate love, fuelled by ambition. It's a classic story really, but a kind of removed duet, as the freshly-loved-up yuppie couple – played by Joni and Don Henley – give individual and detached third-person descriptions of themselves and their power-hungry climb.

Henley here returned to the fold after the 1982 faux pas which saw him replaced by Lionel Richie on 'You Dream Flat Tires' and left purely accidentally uninformed of such. On 'Snakes and Ladders', Henley's work is understated but undeniable. The entire track is high-class nuance all the way, not least of all Mike Landau's chic backwards-reverb guitar that introduces every chorus – a phe*no*menal touch.

The fairly straight-ahead rock rhythm carrying the story of passion going sour was simple, despite the *New York Times* in 1988 describing it as 'A densely textured musical play'. They also got the male character mixed up with the new face that catches the female's eye, but we'll forgive them for that.

It all goes fine for a while – 'Buy the carphone, call the broker, buy the wife a diamond choker'. But by song's end we get, 'Sell the vineyard, call the lawyer, gather garbage to destroy her'. Ouch! No Hollywood ending here, at least not in the movie cliché sense. But the track *is* taken out with a pure Beach Boys-esque repeating-counterpoint vocal collage a-la 'God Only Knows'. Perhaps not Robert Plant's style, but he surely must've kicked himself missing out on writing a lyric over this track which was conceived for his possible gestation.

'The Reoccurring Dream' (Joni Mitchell, Larry Klein)

We're deep in hardcore *Chalk Mark* now. One of Joni's goals for the album was to see how far she could take overlapping choral work without it becoming cacophony. Examples of this inhabited many of the songs, but the experiment reached its peak here. The idea was partly inspired by a specific scene in Mozart's comic opera *The Marriage of Figaro*, where more and more servants appear singing different melodies. But rather than being like the opera – an exercise in morality – this lyric was a commentary on advertising, even brainwashing. It exposed the weakness we all have when faced with the lure of a shiny thing. In more than one way it shared that conceptual theme with 'Snakes and Ladders'. It also re-energised the vain 'Sweet Bird' beauty jar promises and the elusive dreams and vague desires of 'Fiction', bringing the entire collective idea to a climax with a gradually intensifying crescendo of spoken catchphrases, enticements and bribes.

One critic claimed the song exemplified Joni losing her melody mojo, and proved the new brat-pack of female singer-songwriters – like the mellow Suzanne Vega and the casual Tracy Chapman – had seized her throne. This despite the fact the piece was basically a jazz-fusion social-comment collage – a galaxy away from both Chapman's everyman diary snapshots and Vega's intellectual playlets. The criticism fell flat. Neither of those qualities existed in 'The Reoccurring Dream'. As cerebral as it certainly was, intuition was its impulse; the intuition that kicks in – whether for or against – when something is hawked at us. In a way, collage is analogous to musical counterpoint – a collection of interacting elements. In audio collage, melody in the traditional sense has nothing to do with it. Having said that, the existing melodies were quite beautiful, though they did mostly stop short of development after one or two phrases. It was this feeling the critics were most likely picking up on. But they forgot that collage is about other things.

In this case, one of those other things was humour. The catchphrases were certainly humorous, as was what I construed as a nod of appreciation to Thomas Dolby in the way Joni sung the line, 'We can solve everything in science. *Science!*'. That would add a happy coda to their story.

'A Bird That Whistles (Corrina, Corrina)' (Traditional)

This traditional, first recorded in 1928 by Mississippi bluesman, Bo Carter, was one of Joni and Larry's first recordings, and dates from the *Wild Things Run Fast* era. The instrumentation was kept simple, as electric bass, acoustic guitar, vocal, and Wayne Shorter's soprano saxophone. He was instructed to play like a bird and proceeded to knock out nine takes of increasing beauty and complexity. The first two licks – starting at 1m:21s – were the first notes he played. The rest were compiled from the takes, ultimately ending in a flurry of lines from simultaneous takes. If you listen in headphones, at the end you can hear Shorter laughing, actual birdsong, and a passing helicopter – the beat of various wings, closing the discography's '80s era.

Night Ride Home (1991)

Personnel:
Vocals, Guitar, Keyboards, Percussion, Billatron, Oboe, Omnichord: Joni Mitchell
Backing vocals: David Baerwald, Karen Peris, Brenda Russell
Bass: Larry Klein
Drums: Vinnie Colaiuta
Soprano saxophone: Wayne Shorter
Guest lead vocal: David Baerwald
Guitar: Bill Dillon, Larry Klein, Michael Landau
Keyboards: Larry Klein
Pedal steel: Bill Dillon
Percussion: Alex Acuna, Larry Klein
Recorded 1989-Summer 1990 at A&M Studios, One On One, The Kiva, Los Angeles, CA.
Producers: Joni Mitchell and Larry Klein
Engineers: Steve Churchyard, Kristen Connelly, Richard Cottrell, Paula 'Max' Garcia, Jim Hill, Julie Last, Henry Lewy, Dan Marnien, Tony Phillips, Bob Voght
Arranger: Jeremy Lubbock
Label: Geffen
US Release date: 19 February 1991. UK Release date: February 1991.
Chart placings: US: 41, UK: 25, CA: 29, AU: 55, NZ: 40, SE: 43.

Radio Poetry

Legal issues and poor health had made the '80s difficult, to say the least. Joni described herself as then being 'Like a prisoner of war in a climate of distrust'. But things were looking up. In January 1989, *Chalk Mark in a Rain Storm* received a Grammy nomination for Best Female Pop Vocal Performance – her first since that for *The Hissing of Summer Lawns* in 1977. Breaking her habit of avoiding such events, she even attended the ceremony on Wednesday 22 February at L.A.'s Shrine Auditorium.

In March in New York, Joni recorded her part for 'The Spirit of the Forest', a UK benefit single for the preservation of the Brazilian rainforests, written by British-based American producer, Kenny Young, co-writer of '60s pop standard, 'Under the Boardwalk'.

Looking forward, the '90s were a fresh sheet of paper and Joni approached the decade with optimism. On Saturday 21 July 1990, she appeared singing 'Goodbye Blue Sky' in Roger Waters' multi-artist spectacle, *The Wall – Live in Berlin,* performed near Berlin's Brandenburg Gate. Then it was back to L.A. to complete the new album which was slated to be titled either *Night Ride Home* or *Radio Poetry*.

The approach this time was for a pared-down, almost *Hejira*-type sound with acoustic guitar and voice prominent. With the exception of guitarist Michael Landau on the *Two Grey Rooms* instrumental track recorded in 1982, guitar mostly came via Bill Dillon, whom Larry Klein had met on a session for Robbie

Robertson's self-titled 1987 album. Joni jokingly referred to the Billatron, which was Dillon's atmospheric parts sampled and then manipulated through her keyboard performance. Rather than credit herself with the vague liner note description of 'keyboards' when samples were used, she chose instead to bypass technical talk and use actual instrument names such as for the oboe on 'The Only Joy In Town'.

Harmonically, the mood was kept mostly major and positive, with the exception of 'The Windfall'. Some dark subject matter prevailed, but any minor chord passages were balanced by a major-key redemption.

In order to avoid a particular mood being prolonged from song to song, in the vicinity of 100 song combinations were auditioned. Likewise, any track that appeared to kill off the one before was a no-no. In the end, it was felt that even the final track flowed back to the first quite naturally.

David Geffen was certainly happy. He was enthused enough to say, 'Oh, this is great. This could've come right after *Hejira*'. He was particularly pleased with the lyrics being so conspicuous and easily heard. Unfortunately, the label didn't wish to finance the amount of videos Joni had in mind, so she took the responsibility upon herself using proceeds from sales of her paintings at London and Edinburgh exhibitions. No label authorisation for videos meant the traditional mainstream broadcast outlets were off the table, so effort was put into promoting to small TV stations, who were happy to take them on.

Due to health concerns and her voice needing a rest, Joni chose not to tour the album. The unavailability of her drummer Vinnie Coliauta – busy working with Sting – was another reason. Instead, she made key promo radio and TV appearances in the USA and England. In May 1991 in Saskatoon, she spoke at the annual conference for the Canada Council of the Arts. Their theme was 'How to make Van Goghs', to which Joni's argument was, 'A lot of great art comes out of mental disturbance. How are you gonna teach *that?*'.

Otherwise, a lot of time was spent at home in L.A., even though Joni still struggled to think of the city as home. In 1990 she told a *Vox* interviewer, 'I don't think we'll ever get out of there. But it's like that song of Don Henley's, 'Sunset Grill'. The last line is the reason we stay – 'All our friends are here''.

'Night Ride Home' (Joni Mitchell)

Released as a CD single and 7" single A-side, February 1991 (US and UK), b/w 'Slouching Towards Bethlehem'.

The title song and first single, originally known as 'Fourth of July Night Ride Home', was certainly autobiographical and conceived after a late-night drive home to their rented house with private beach in Hawaii on Independence Day, 1987. Joni has described it as one of those magical nights sprinkled with fairy dust when even the highway's white line was alluring. But there was more to the night. Earlier they'd noticed their private beach being invaded by the neighbours who were having a barbecue and letting off fireworks. Not planning to use the beach that night, they let it go. But returning home, they found the bed soaked with water and moved to the middle of the room, and a big hole in the roof. A note left by the neighbour said, 'Gee, your roof caught fire. We don't know how it happened. But we had a spare key from last year and brought the garden hose over. Hope you don't mind.'. They had, of course, caused the fire.

The song was tested on the *Chalk Mark* European promo tour, first in Paris and then live on the UK TV show, *Wired*, on Friday 20 May 1988. In general, people took to the song immediately. It was short, cinematic, and its simple-as-could-be chord pattern communicated directly to a listener. With a newly-pared-back spacious aesthetic such as this, an inspired word twist easily gained attention.

Round the curve
And a big dark horse
Red taillights on his hide
Is keeping right alongside
Rev for stride

Recorded at The Kiva, the track featured the absorbing sound of a real cricket that hid behind a curtain for a few nights, unable to be caught.

'Passion Play (When All the Slaves Are Free)' (Joni Mitchell)

Then suddenly we were in serious territory. Considering how the press would often jump to conclusions where Joni was concerned, the tactic of viewing Christ's final era through the prism of the traditional German *Passion Play* was a smart move. Otherwise, it could've been far too easy to presume her to be born again and forget that her material was often a form of theatre. In interviews around this time, she had declared herself to be a yoga practitioner with an interest in Buddhism. The track's underlying tabla rhythm throughout certainly threw your ears out of the Middle East, far further east to the Subcontinent. The combination showed an open mind.

In complete contrast to a lyric focus, Joni and Larry performed a virtually wordless early version of the song on *Rai 1 TV* in San Remo, Italy, on Saturday 22 October 1988, when she was presented with the Tenco Songwriter Award for significant contributions to the field. Singing predominantly in vowel sounds, she allowed for one line that never made it to the final lyric; 'It'll take time, but time brings changes'.

The instrumental alone was impressive enough, certainly on the album where it was enhanced by guitarist Bill Dillon's appropriately passionate hovering aurora. But whatever the lyrical meaning, the music itself emitted that timeless undeniable quality of heart that spoke directly to you, in such a way that perhaps we hadn't heard since *Hejira*.

'Cherokee Louise' (Joni Mitchell)

On contemplating the mountain of injustice that had stacked up against her in recent years, Joni was suddenly struck by the greatest injustice of all – that which befell her friend as a thirteen-year-old here named Cherokee Louise. Molested by a foster-family member, the girl fled from her home and hid in the tunnels under Saskatoon's Broadway Bridge for several days. No one would take her in. Tragically, through no fault of her own, she was sent to prison – a detail absent from the lyric.

A crack of light shone through the lyric with the friends placing pennies on the railroad tracks just days before. Soon they were reading comics under the bridge, while out in the world the police searched for the girl. The below highly-crafted stanza further pushed home the background reality.

Ever since we turned thirteen
It's like a minefield
Walking to the door
Going out you get the third degree
And comin' in you get the third world war

Most moving of all perhaps were Wayne Shorter's joyful soprano sax figures, the fine lines separating the story's virtuous and sinister layers.

This lyric houses a line that, at first, I questioned craft-wise. Some investigation revealed the method in Joni's madness. The line was, 'The place where you can stand, and press your hands like it was bubblebath, in dust piled high as me'. Surely the logical order of events would be, 'The place where you can stand and press your hands in dust piled high as me like it was bubblebath'. It comes off as a forced rhyme, where 'me' is made to align with the following 'street'. It wasn't imperative that the two lines rhymed unless she wanted the rhyme scheme to match across the entire song, which appeared to be the case. The inner rhyme of 'stand/hands' also had to exist to match the 'time/climb' of the earlier equivalent section. But what was the explanation for dropping the technique like a hot stone in the equivalent position on the later verse line, 'She runs home to her foster Dad, he opens up a zipper'? Therein lay the true skill that caused all these moves to make sense. That line's implication – certainly the most critical line of the entire album – was clearly so important that Joni was prepared to potentially forego even her own artistic integrity for the cause. The detail of the earlier patterns and the ambiguity of the 'bubblebath' line, were an intricate show to emphasise their absence once it all fell away — Lyric-writing of an intensely high order. The dedication to tradition was admirable, even more the willingness to break tradition.

'The Windfall (Everything For Nothing)' (Joni Mitchell)

Joni rightfully went for the jugular here, specifically that of her housekeeper and the unjust lawsuit wrought by that individual. Other situations likely played a part of course – as we know, lyric ideas for a song often came from multiple sources. But this lyric possibly suffered a little due to an obvious overtone of hopelessness, not to mention writer proximity to the subject. If you weren't aware of the personal situation upon first hearing the song – and let's face it, most people weren't – as a listener, the complaints were difficult to justify to yourself. I just overlooked it at the time as it was possible that I could've had the wrong idea.

The instrumental track, though finely performed, lacked excitement compared to what preceded it, as if less thought out. But that *was* the idea for *Night Ride Home* after all – more intuition and less overt planning. In fact, lyric notwithstanding, the track came across like a light-relief buffer between the heavier subject matter that bookended it. Despite my quibbling, pearls of insight were never far from the surface in any of this material, and this song was worth it, if only for the below stanza of snarly humour.

In the land of mass frustration
The judges are sleeping
Counting woolly little lawyers
And grinding their teeth

'Slouching Towards Bethlehem' (Joni Mitchell – Lyric adapted from 'The Second Coming' by W.B. Yeats)

Released as a CD and single B-side, 1991 (US), February 1991 (UK), b/w 'Night Ride Home'.
Released as a single B-side, 1991 (DE), b/w 'Come In From the Cold (Edit)'.

Ohio-born singer/songwriter, David Baerwald, recorded his 1990 album *Bedtime Stories* at The Kiva with Larry Klein at the helm. For years Baerwald had attempted to set to music, Irish poet W.B. Yeats' 1919 work, *The Second Coming.* Attempts were fruitless, so Joni took it upon herself to restructure the text into a singable lyric. Much of the original poem survived the transference while other parts were adapted. The third verse – from 'Hoping and hoping' to 'Troubling my eyes' – was Joni's work, which she tried to keep in the style of the first.

The track, which acted as the album's nerve centre, was virtually complete before they asked for permission to use the poetry. The Yeats estate had a policy of only allowing use for classical music settings. But the song was sent away with the request, and breath was held. Happily, the request was accepted, the only condition being that they use the phrase 'Adapted by' in the credits.

The final mix was percussive and darkly beautiful. For all that it perfectly captured the poem's ominous mood, Larry Klein's taut fretless bass spirals – such as at 5m:05s – added a tear-inducing pathos. Contributing to all this was the house cat, El Cafe, whose sampled meow had sat in the Fairlight for some time waiting for a suitable home. It can be heard slowed down to an evil growl at 3m:09s after the words 'head like a lion'.

Recording was completed in June 1990, mere months in advance of the Gulf War's commencement, after which the richly-textured track acquired a raw resonance.

'Come In From the Cold' (Joni Mitchell)

Released as a single A-side (Edit), July 1991 (UK), b/w 'Ray's Dad's Cadillac'. CA: 27.
Released as a CD single (Edit), 1991 (UK), b/w 'Ray's Dad's Cadillac' and 'Come In From the Cold (LP)'.
Released as a single A-side (Edit), 1991 (DE), b/w 'Slouching Towards Bethlehem'.

Joni lost her voice after performing the multiple takes it took to achieve this final vocal. But it was worth it for the performance they ended up with. It stuck out for a lot of the label people. With talk of it being a single, Joni was against cutting it in length. But by Christmas 1990 – five months after the recording was complete – when the album was delivered to the label, enough time had passed for her to be objective about where to cut it. She approached it in the sense of making the single like a trailer for a movie. More than half the 7m:30s track was cut for the single, leaving only verses one, three and four of seven, which was extreme. But it was enough to achieve a Top 30 hit in Canada – Joni's biggest there since 'In France They Kiss On Main Street' in 1976. That a self-critical song seriously addressing the journey from youth to middle-age – expressed over a repeated single-section folk-form minus a significant chorus – could be a radio hit, seems almost unbelievable now. But there it stood riding the airwaves, a rare and beautiful beast.

'Nothing Can Be Done' (Joni Mitchell, Larry Klein)

The only Mitchell/Klein collaboration present was born from a jam Larry had with guitarist, Bill Dillon. It was recorded when they met at a session for Robert Robertson's self-titled 1987 debut album. That jam brought Dillon into Joni's orbit. He was invited to the house, she wrote some words, and the track became 'Nothing Can Be Done'.

Like 'Come In from the Cold', the lyric theme was the onset of middle-age. Some inspiration came from the 1927 Max Ehrmann prose poem, 'The Desiderata of Happiness'. That piece had already inspired two pop recordings. The first came in 1970 as 'Go Placidly' by ex-The-Nice drummer Brian Davison. The following year, the song, under the title 'Desiderata', was a spoken-word global hit for American TV chat show host, Les Crane.

Bill Dillon's shimmering lead guitar work truly enhanced the understated backing track, which was the album's primary expose of his abilities. Also involved was Klein's recent production client, singer/songwriter David Baerwald, who contributed a vocal. In the spirit of *Chalk Mark in a Rain Storm*, his vocal was an added counterpoint, as opposed to making the song an out-'n'-out duet.

'Nothing Can Be Done' fulfilled a similar function to side one's 'The Windfall', by supplying some level of conventional relief between sets of emotionally demanding, though undeniably rewarding and substantial songs.

'The Only Joy In Town' (Joni Mitchell)

By this point, the album was ready for more levity. Not that it was an issue – the contrast of mood and rhythm between tracks so far was finely-balanced, and unsurprisingly so considering the time Joni had put in to perfect the song sequence.

Rome's Spanish Steps were here the setting for the admiration of a costumed flower child getting all the attention amongst the 'deadpan sidewalk vendors'. 'In my youth, I would have followed him, all through this terracotta town'. The vocal delivery was cheerful, making this as positive a vehicle as the title song.

In hindsight, the key discussion point here is the technology used. A Fairlight CMI oboe sample added to the 18th-century classical overtone, sounding even 20th-century neo-classical in the abstract line at 2m:09s. Joni played the part, crediting herself with oboe instead of keyboards. She had a point with her argument that even though someone else played the original oboe note, it was *her* manipulating it musically. To her, it was the musical idea that mattered. In 1990, samples were considered just another relevant tool, before the 21st-century purist wheel-reinvention backlash.

By and large, this track's samples were finely applied, in an era when sample quality was still given some leeway. The oboe sample loop (used to artificially create note sustain) is detectable on some held notes, causing them to sound perfectly in tune and therefore slightly inauthentic. But hearing that now is just the price you pay for the relentless technology juggernaut. This recording's techniques can hardly be blamed for not being up to the development in those that came after.

'Ray's Dad's Cadillac' (Joni Mitchell)

Released as a single B-side, July 1991 (UK), b/w 'Come In From the Cold (Edit)'.
Released as a CD single, 1991 (UK), b/w 'Come In From the Cold (Edit)' and 'Come In From the Cold (LP)'.

Without a doubt, the album's most accessible track, this recollection of late-1950s teenage recreation could've possibly fared better chart-wise than its cooler A-side. Vocalist, Brenda Russell, added some extra R&B cachet as if to hint at doo-wop. Wayne Shorter's soprano sax splashed pointillist exclamations around the scenery, which – along with Larry Klein's elegant fretless bass glides – gave the track additional meat for anyone needing more than a cheerful singalong.

'Two Grey Rooms' (Joni Mitchell)

In 1989, Joni resurrected the *Wild Things Run Fast* instrumental known as 'Speechless'. She finally hit on a suitable lyric concept – the story of a German aristocrat who took up drab rooms just so he could watch a long-lost lover walk to and from work every day. Joni placed herself front-and-centre as the narrator. The intro's wordless vocals remained from the 1982 recording, which was now filled out with an orchestral arrangement courtesy of Jeremy Lubbock. A promo film was shot and included in the 1991 video compilation, *Come In from the Cold*.

Turbulent Indigo (1994)

Personnel:
Vocals, Guitar, Keyboards, Percussion, Billatron: Joni Mitchell
Backing vocals: Kris Kello, Charles Valentino
Bass, Organ: Larry Klein
Drums: Jim Keltner, Carlos Vega
Guest vocals: Seal ('How Do You Stop')
Guitar: Michael Landau, Steuart Smith
Pedal steel: Greg Leisz
Soprano saxophone: Wayne Shorter
Synthesizer, Guitorgan: Bill Dillon
Recorded in 1993 at The Kiva, Los Angeles, CA.
Producers: Joni Mitchell, Larry Klein
Engineers: Dan Marnien, Julie Last, Paul Lundin, Paula 'Max' Schape,
Label: Reprise
US Release date: 25 October 1994. UK Release date: October 1994.
Chart placings: US: 47, UK: 53, CAN: 24

Contrary to what we think might play out were a married couple to split, move into different houses, and start recording an album together the next day, Joni and Larry dealt with that situation admirably. They've both said that, if anything, it made for better work decisions. All sessions took place at Joni's home studio, The Kiva, and the album was initially conceived as a swansong for release on Geffen Records under the title *Swansong*. That is until Warner Brothers Records president, Mo Ostin, caught wind of it and declared his enthusiasm to have her back on Reprise Records. After the success of *Night Ride Home*, there was a buzz for the new record – something Joni had barely ever sensed in advance of an album, if only because she was always looking ahead.

But the times were catching up. An album of songs touching on political and domestic violence with side-turns into social chastening and religious rebellion was almost unadventurous by 1994 standards, but therefore more acceptable to the mainstream. Like those of the prior album, the *Turbulent Indigo* arrangements were sparse, allowing the lyrics more front-and-centre impact.

In May 1994, Joni appeared accompanied by traditional Irish group, The Chieftains, Wayne Shorter, and Japanese guitarist, Hotei Tomoyasu, at the Aoniyoshi Festival in Nara, Japan. In August she performed at Canada's Edmonton Folk Music Festival for the first time in decades. Otherwise, appearances were predominantly promotional interviews and limited to California and parts of Canada, taking place throughout September and October. The album release party was held on Monday 24 October as a meet-and-greet for invited guests at Santa Monica's Ruth Bloom Art Gallery, where they could listen while viewing 30 of Joni's paintings on exhibit. A media showcase and press conference followed on Sunday 13 November at 41 Queensgate Terrace in London.

An early American edition of the CD came with a miniature tin ear as a kind of self-deprecating Vincent Van Gogh joke to align with the cover's self-portrait. But all humour aside, *Turbulent Indigo* deservedly won Pop Album of the Year and Best Album Package at the 1996 Grammy Awards ceremony on Wednesday 28 February.

'Sunny Sunday' (Joni Mitchell)

Released as CD single, 1994.

Turbulent Indigo comfortably resumed the stately orientation proffered by *Night Ride Home*. From the opening lines, 'She pulls the shade, It's just another sunny Sunday', it was all there; the translucence, the turbulence and the instrumental delicacy combined with lyrical dismissal of compromise. This concentration further secured the commitment of longtime fans and confirmed the devotion of new ones. For many, Joni's music was now nothing short of a religion. But as she pointed out at the time, church music would never go near the augmented-4th Devil's interval, which she smoothly sneaked in at the lines, 'That one little victory, that's all she needs'.

This character sketch outlined a friend of a friend and her daily routine of standing at her front door taking pot-shots at the streetlight. 'But the day she hits, that's the day she'll leave'. The lyric compared the friend to Blanche DuBois, the central character from the famed Tennessee Williams' play, *A Streetcar Named Desire.*

Perhaps not as gleaming as the opening of *Night Ride Home*, 'Sunny Sunday' was buoyant compared to some avenues *Turbulent Indigo* would tread. Business as usual for Joni Mitchell. If you got the dark, you also got the light. Indeed the song's closing was almost humorous in its resignation; 'She pulls the shade, it's just another sunny Monday' – and the cycle repeated.

'Sex Kills' (Joni Mitchell)

Released as CD single, 1994. CA: 68.

Sunday 3 May 1992, the final night of the L.A. riots. Driving through Brentwood, Los Angeles, Joni pulled up behind a Cadillac that had the license plate 'JUST ICE'. Whether the vehicle belonged to New York rapper, Joseph Williams Jr. aka Just-Ice, would remain a mystery. It could've been a member of the public making a statement. If it wasn't, Joni certainly ran with it; 'Is justice just ice? Governed by greed and lust?'. The event pulled the curtain open on a raft of society's ills that spilled into the lyric as if uncontrollably.

Doctors pills give you brand new ills
And the bills bury you like an avalanche
Oh and the tragedies in the nurseries

Little kids packin' guns to school
The ulcerated ozone
These tumours of the skin

The list of concerns engulfed the song as if no amount of orderly technique would make any difference. But the poetic teasers were radiant.

Lawyers haven't been this popular since Robespierre slaughtered half of France

This hostile sun beating down on this massive mess we're in

The chorus continued as a random list if you read the lines 'And the gas leaks, and the oil spills' as compound nouns. Even the title 'Sex Kills' could be viewed that way. But if you saw each pair's second word as a verb, the depth and significance became obvious.

A barrage of distorted guitar intensified as the track progressed. But the most powerful way to hear the song appeared to be live. Joni gave a compelling solo rendition on *The Tonight Show with Jay Leno* in 1995. The full live band experience with drummer Brian Blade, pedal steel player, Greg Leisz, and Larry Klein, brought an urgent alt-country jazz-fusion amalgam to the table, suggesting nothing short of genre innovation could get this message across. For that aural treat, consult the 1998 concert DVD, *Painting With Words and Music*.

'Sex Kills' was serious stuff with a lyric that pulled no punches, and it even made Canada's RPM 100. To top that, Bob Dylan loved the song. Nothing to sneeze at, even for his equal.

'How Do You Stop' (Dan Hartman, Charlie Midnight)

Released as a CD single, 1994, b/w 'The Sire of Sorrow (Job's Sad Song)' and 'Moon at the Window (Live)'. UK: 100. CA: 56.

First recorded by James Brown for his hit 1986 album *Gravity*, it was his live version of 'How Do You Stop' from the 1987 *James Brown and Friends* Detroit show that turned Joni's head enough to cover the song. 'If I Could', her duet with British singer/songwriter, Seal, appeared on his *Seal II* earlier in 1994, his appearance with Joni on 'How Do You Stop' a reciprocal record company arrangement. But this was less of a duet and more Seal on backing vocals with a few improvised hollers here and there. On any duet, Joni never seemed quite prepared to hand over the reins for very long.

The song was the catalyst for another of the weird coincidences that punctuated her career. After singing it along with a couple of others at an Eric Anderson concert at The Cave in L.A., she and Larry accepted Eric's invitation to meet at his hotel for a party later. They waited in the downstairs lobby for some time. On the stairs, Joni bumped into a guy who exclaimed, 'Aaah Joni Mitchell!'. When she asked what he was doing there, he said he wrote songs for other people. When asked who, he answered 'James Brown'. Telling him she'd just sung 'How Do You Stop' that night, the guy said, 'I wrote that song!'. He was the song's co-writer, Charlie Midnight. Further to that, the song's other writer, Dan Hartman, had died tragically earlier in 1994 at the age of 43.

Brown's R&B hit appealed to Joni. But in the context of *Turbulent Indigo*, it was going to be working hard to compete with the captivating title track that came hot on its heels.

'Turbulent Indigo' (Joni Mitchell)

The title song's emotion was deep-seated and the lyric made a brutal point. In the early '90s, Joni had been invited back to Saskatoon to speak at a conference of the Canadian Council of the Arts. The theme was 'Making Van Goghs'. The council were fostering an assembly-line approach to making art, which rubbed Joni completely the wrong way. She opened her talk by saying, 'You cannot make Van Goghs. Artists can be encouraged or even groomed but not manufactured. Art is the result of experience, and Van Gogh's despair and suicide are not what you want to duplicate.'. Thus the prominent line, 'Oh what do you know about living in turbulent indigo?'.

The title itself referred not only to Van Gogh's disturbed mental state and colourings, but paint pigment itself, which he is known to have attempted to eat at one point. The lyric emphasises the tourists as they are guided by the roped-off paintings, 'Talking about the madhouse, Talking about the ear'. Then the brutal reality hits home.

> The madman hangs in fancy homes they wouldn't let him near
> He'd piss in their fireplace
> He'd drag them through turbulent indigo

The last verse was adapted almost entirely from Van Gogh quotes, the most telling of which was the following. 'One may have a blazing hearth in one's soul and yet no one ever came to sit by it. Passers-by see only a wisp of smoke from the chimney and continue on their way'.

'Last Chance Lost' (Joni Mitchell)

It's tempting to think of 'Last Chance Lost' as a description of Joni and Larry's marriage ending. But if I did that, I'd be going against my earlier warning to be wary of reading too much autobiography into any of these lyrics. Some view the song as dark and even the album's most hopeless statement. But knowing of the couple's amicable split, I read the lyric as a resigned and matter-of-fact reality check. These two were perfectly able to 'Bicker on the rifle range' (probably the *last* place you'd want to) without losing control.

The virtually acoustic track resonated with finality and frailty, not least of all from the guitar's gorgeous low B flat string seeming as if it might snap at

1m:22s, adding a loose world music inflection to the instrument. But there was more. This turbulent world's deepest hollows were still to be accessed.

'The Magdalene Laundries' (Joni Mitchell)

Joni's songs were now often written in the daytime. These chord changes came outside in the sun, sitting on a rock, attuned to the sounds and bird calls of British Columbia. Visiting the supermarket, she bought a newspaper – *The Vancouver Sun* – something she rarely did. She didn't even get past the front-page story of a Dublin nunnery, The Sisters of Our Lady of Charity. They'd sold eleven acres to a developer who, upon ploughing in preparation for building, found well over one hundred unmarked graves. From the 19th century on, most Irish nunneries, and many in other countries, had within them a Magdalene laundry – a place where so-called fallen women were incarcerated and forced to labour, often taken there by their own families. It could be for prostitution, unwed pregnancy, or merely being unmarried, attractive and walking around.

The first-person lyric was the voice of one of these women, speaking from within her prison. After writing the song, Joni contacted Irish recording artist, Sinead O'Connor, with a view to her possibly performing it. Coincidentally, O'Connor had been sent to that very laundry herself as a young teenager. Quite incredibly, that workhouse wasn't shut down until 1996, two years after this song's release.

The arrangement was left basically as acoustic guitar and fretless bass, backed by deep vistas of synth and/or Billatron. But as powerful as this version was, Joni's emotionally searing recording of the song with traditional Irish group, The Chieftains, for their 1999 album *Tears of Stone*, trumped it hands down. It's well worth a listen. Once the pairing of the two acts has pushed you to the precipice, the addition of evocative backing vocals from Irish sister group, Screaming Orphans, pushes you over the edge, finishing the job.

'Not To Blame' (Joni Mitchell)

At this point in the album, the return of Joni's exploratory piano-playing was welcome. *Night Ride Home* had only one example of it in the 1982 'Two Grey Rooms' backing track. That made 'Not To Blame' the first Joni piano we'd really heard since 'Ethiopia' on *Dog Eat Dog*.

The blend of piano, heart-warming pedal steel chords and melodic soprano sax lines expressed sympathy for the lyric's harsh domestic violence reality. Some thought it referred to the recent Nicole Brown Simpson murder case, which was fresh and raw in everyone's mind, but it was in fact, written well before that event. Rather, it was specific to the violent situations many women suffered, and even correlated with the unfortunate victims of 'The Magdalene Laundries' in the line, 'Not one wet eye around her lonely little grave'.

'Borderline' (Joni Mitchell)

'Borderline' is five minutes of real refinement that expresses its profound meaning with simplicity. It even breaks into an almost country and western purity in the vocal delivery of 'Like a barbed wire fence' – a style allusion absent from Joni's music for quite some time. Where 'Not To Blame' had an overtone of sympathy, 'Borderline' had one of melancholy tragedy – the tragedy that occurs when selfishness and class structure render an entire species unaware of the damage it causes itself.

All things being relative, a reflection on the human social divide would likely come across as light fare after the darker realities of the prior two songs. The lyric explored (or maybe deplored) the myriad situations that humans allow to cause psychological or even physical separation – from judgment and humiliation to nationalism and religion. In a 2015 interview, Joni spoke of the pecking order of smart and dumb that the Japanese derive from blood-type. She had once been asked if she was A-type, which was said to be smart blood. Her point with the lyric was that one way or another, humans will always pull rank against each other, whether by blood-type or principle.

The line, 'Every swan caught on the grass will draw a borderline,' came from an experience she had on New York's Long Island, where some motorists had pulled over to view a swan caught on the roadside, protecting her babies. There the lyric's theme crossed over to the animal kingdom. Not to mention the brute present who drew his own borderline via an obvious belligerent attitude toward the animals. We can be sure he was responsible for Joni's snarl on the line 'Every mean-street's kick-ass', immediately preceding the swan line's graceful delivery.

The track was included in the 2014 box set; *Love Has Many Faces*, featuring a newly-recorded overdub from American trumpet player, Ambrose Akinmusire.

'Yvette in English' (Joni Mitchell, David Crosby)

The first song born for *Turbulent Indigo* was co-written with David Crosby via fax machine. Both his original lyric draft and Joni's first development differed extremely from the final result. Certain motifs, like 'Tongues', 'Picasso' and 'Cigarette burns', were Crosby's and present from the beginning. He had a line, 'The night has oozed into electric cafes', which was a cue that likely led to Joni's 'Uninsulated wires laid bare' with its metaphor recalling the problematic fuse boards of the *For the Roses* track, 'Electricity'.

Originally, Crosby had asked Joni to produce a track for his current album in the works. Not feeling she could, they agreed on a writing collaboration instead. The original version was on his album *Thousand Roads*, released almost 18 months prior to *Turbulent Indigo*.

The lyric covered the brief encounter in a Left Banke cafe between a French woman, Yvette, and a man who struggled with her native tongue. A synthesizer with subtle accordion tonality evoked the scene, while the lyric's 'Bony bridge between left and right' matched it visually. Saxophonist Wayne Shorter drew in close, his solo lines resembling the topple of a foot auditioning a high-heeled shoe, something Joni said she would've reflected visually were the track to have a video.

'Yvette in English' was the album's lightest, most carefree moment, its painterly aspect more than worthy of the accompanying overcast canvases.

'The Sire of Sorrow (Job's Sad Song)' (Joni Mitchell)

In the Old Testament's *Book of Job,* Job was beset by tragedy and bad health. But he remained faithful to God despite being at a loss to justify the circumstances. Given the opportunity to question it, he kept silent. In 'The Sire of Sorrow', Joni Mitchell had no such reserve.

Why have you soured and curdled me?
What have I done to you?
That you make everything I dread and everything I fear come true?

Having survived her negative experience of the '80s, she found herself cheerful enough to tackle a lyric of such religious depth. Intending to mine the psalms for inspiration, the *Book of Job* sidetracked her. Acquiring the St. James, New Jerusalem and Gideon texts, she went about the lyric, restructuring the ancient verses, paraphrasing occasionally but without disturbing the general idea.

Keeping in mind the possibility of artistic license and fiction in the lyric, verse two appeared to address Joni's career.

Kings heard my words and they sought out my company
But now the janitors of Shadowland flick their brooms at me

The phrase 'Pompous physicians' referred to her own health battles, the lyric as a whole to many forms of injustice. That notion was palpable when she played the new recording for an ex-policeman who'd recently sniffed out something rotten in the force. All he'd gotten for his trouble was the murder of his family.

Bible adaptation or not, the inherent rage was electric. The musical arrangement maintained the album's general approach of acoustic guitar, fretless bass and percussion, intermittently flooded with Bill Dillon's cascading synthetic guitar washes. Joni's perpetually interrupting multi-vocal choir of antagonists declared itself with the theatrical power of Prince vocal-blocks but might've worked more successfully sung by other individuals. The entire seven minutes conspired to make an album-ending more formally compelling than any since 'Shadows and Light' on *The Hissing of Summer Lawns*, or maybe even as far back as the *For the Roses* closer, 'Judgement of the Moon and Stars'. And like the lyric of the former, the text was left to lie unresolved.

Contemporary Tracks

'It's All Over Now, Baby Blue (Demo)' (Bob Dylan)
Released in the box set Joni Mitchell: The Complete Geffen Recordings, 2003.

This features the distinctive synthesizer sound Joni named 'Presbyterian in

Peru', found on 'Cool Water' from *Chalk Mark in a Rain Storm*. But for my money, the overall sound, playing style and vocal phrasing places this recording fairly and squarely in the *Turbulent Indigo* era. It even shares a vocal turn with, and alters a chord move to sound exactly like, part of 'The Sire of Sorrow'. Unless of course, that track took cues from this recording.

Taming the Tiger (1998)

Personnel:
Vocals, Bass, Guitar, Keyboards, Percussion: Joni Mitchell
Bass: Larry Klein
Drums: Brian Blade
Guitar: Michael Landau
Pedal Steel: Greg Leisz
Saxophone: Wayne Shorter
Spoken vocals: Femi Jiya
Trumpet: Mark Isham
Recorded 1994-1998 at The Kiva, Los Angeles, CA.
Producer: Joni Mitchell
Engineers: Femi Jiya, Dan Marnien, Tony Phillips
Label: Reprise
US Release date: 29 September 1998. UK Release date: September 1998.
Chart placings: US: 75. UK: 57. CA: 86. NO: 25.

After the success of *Turbulent Indigo*, Joni Mitchell was big news again. The awards came in their droves. In addition to the 1996 Pop Album of the Year and Best Album Package Grammys, came *Billboard* magazine's 1995 Century Award for distinguished creative achievement; The 1996 Governor General's Performing Arts Award for outstanding body of work and enduring contribution to the performing arts in Canada, and even Sweden's 1996 Polar Music Prize. Not least of all was the 6 May 1997 induction into the Rock and Roll Hall of Fame. Joni sidestepped the ceremony held at the Renaissance Hotel in Cleveland, Ohio. Graham Nash accepted on her behalf, holding onto the award for a year, presenting it to her before a live audience at the recording of her private concerts for the *Painting Words and Music* live DVD. This was filmed over the two nights of 29 and 30 May 1998 at Warner Brothers Studios in Burbank, CA.

Joni's attitude to any award was realistic. She explained to *Mojo* magazine in 1998.

> It's not really rarefied. The best records don't make record of the year, the best records do not win the Grammys. The best do not win, so all this is perpetuating the falseness of the victors, you know? It's not correcting history as it should be.

With all the attention, it was only a matter of time before something of Joni's got the remix treatment in the fashion of the day. This occurred with Robin Goodfellow's 1995 Reprise Records CD single of seven 'Big Yellow Taxi' remixes. It was respectable work and Joni gave her approval. In 1997, Janet Jackson (Featuring Q-Tip) sampled the song in the worldwide hit, 'Got 'Til It's Gone'. But *that* track was flimsy at best, and aside from the 'Big Yellow Taxi' sample, barely justified itself musically, despite an astonishing *five* additional songwriter credits.

L.A.'s Wiltern Theater was host to the Walden Woods Project benefit concert which on 16 April 1998 saw Joni perform the Arlen/Koehler standard, 'Stormy Weather', with a 60-piece orchestra. In May she performed an historic small seven-concert tour of the West Coast (including Vancouver) with Van Morrison and Bob Dylan. It was a good warm-up for Joni's first headlining tour since 1983, the eleven-date Fall Tour of America which ran from 23 October to 7 November.

Larry Klein remained on bass for the tour. Joni had handled bass duties herself for the album, with the exception of Larry's performances on 'Harlem in Havana', 'Lead Balloon' and 'The Crazy Cries of Love'. As she told her current partner Donald Freed, 'It's not like Larry and I are out of each other's life, we're just out of each other's hair'. Donald replied, 'Write that down, that's another song.'.

'Harlem in Havana' (Joni Mitchell)

Equal-parts teenage emancipation and life-affirming formation, the glorious opener teases like the '50s taboos it celebrates. Joni was an underage teenager when she and a friend secretly attended vaudeville performer Leon Claxton's *Harlem In Havana* revue when it hit Saskatoon. Inside the tent, the two got their first taste of black music and first glimpse of crossdresser burlesque – song material if ever there was.

The track's abstract introduction begins as digital synthesis divided into harmonic frequency-partial overtones, soon enveloped by a feverish modal jazz embellished by saxophonist Wayne Shorter. It sounds fresh to this day, a full seductive minute-and-a-half passing before the vocal even enters. Engineer Femi Jiya's carnival bark and Joni's gritty electric guitar cause the listener to virtually smell the finely hovering sawdust particles.

In many ways the song could act as a good introduction for a new Joni fan, in that it fits alongside other early-life autobiographical tales like 'The Tea Leaf Prophecy' and 'Cherokee Louise' – collected together as they all were on the 2005 compilation, *Songs of a Prairie Girl*. That album effectively told the story that led to all of Joni's music. All her formative experiences played a part in what the compilation and 'Harlem in Havana' eventually became. But even so, as the song says, 'Auntie Ruthie would've cried if she knew we were on the inside'.

'Man From Mars' (Joni Mitchell)

The slow, soothing and spacious Brian Blade drum groove here acts as the basis for guitar and keyboards performed solely by Joni. Asked to write a broken-love song for the 1996 movie, 'Grace of My Heart', she was unsure if she could manufacture such an emotion without a real-life conceptual model. That is until her Abyssinian cat Nietzsche messed on the kitchen floor and was scolded and cast outside, only to disappear for 18 days – the time it took to write the song. Calling for the cat every night, Joni noticed certain sounds in the area for the first time, some of which made it onto the recording.

American actress, Kristen Vigard, sung the original movie version. Joni's vocal on the same backing track accidentally made it onto an early soundtrack edition, an interesting contrast to the more abstract *Taming the Tiger* arrangement. Another interesting contrast is the album version's rolling synth-piano verse figure, identical to – but a tone higher than – the same in 'Dog Eat Dog'.

'Love Puts On a New Face' (Joni Mitchell)

In the course of three verses, we traverse the stages of a relationship, from happiness to argument to separation, represented by what almost felt like a formula now – acoustic guitar, *Turbulent-Indigo*-style synth washes, soprano sax lines and contrasting pedal steel, all beautifully executed of course. But the title hook melody seemed almost thrown away and didn't quite deliver the punch the lyric line deserved – 'But in France they say, every day, love puts on a new face'. But you *could* view that move as a new face in itself, and therefore appropriate.

'Lead Balloon' (Joni Mitchell)

The title cliché was unexpected, but it was memorable and might've had something to do with the song being chosen for radio promotion. In light of that, the opening line was probably risky, but it sure was an attention-getter and worthy of a classic novel opening; '"Kiss my ass," I said, and threw my drink'. The narrator justified her outburst with the line, 'Must be the Irish blood, fight before you think'. We never find out what specifically provoked the reaction, but verse two makes the adversary's character all too clear.

I had to ask him for a helping hand
It came with the heart
Of a Bonaparte
Of a frozen fish

A variety of edgy electric guitars – courtesy of Joni and Mike Landau – set the tone. In the end, it's a rock song we're dealing with – the first such texture since 1988's 'Dancin' Clown' – which makes Wayne Shorter's typical soprano saxophone flair here seem redundant.

The additional musicians notwithstanding, Joni's guitars gave the track the lone-genius feel of a Prince recording – an interesting idea for her, but not one that she developed to any real conclusion.

'No Apologies' (Joni Mitchell)

It feels like the opportunity to spotlight injustice took precedence over song-craft here. The way the opening line lands a weak syllable on a strong beat says it all – 'The general offered no apoloGIES'. Then the same thing occurs two lines later. As relevant as the lyric arguments are, the song falters by merely stating the outrageous but offering no profound elucidation or interpretation, the likes of which would've fallen plentifully onto the page two decades before. The choruses bring no dynamic uplift of any kind, no crescendo building tension, and the song merely ends with a repeat of the opening line. Surrounded by the impassioned nostalgia of 'Harlem in Havana' and the unapologetic flip of 'Taming the Tiger', I must view 'No Apologies' as an also-ran.

'Taming the Tiger' (Joni Mitchell)

The famous quote by actress, Sophia Loren, in regard to fame – 'It's hard to catch and harder still to ride' – completely summed up the title track's theme of frustration with showbiz machinations. It was a semi-return to collage, with a number of quotes that collectively suggested Joni to be so over stoking the star-maker machinery that she'd perhaps become bereft of originality. That was of course untrue. 'Tiger tiger burning bright' was a quote from English poet William Blake's 1794 work, 'The Tyger'. 'The old man is snoring' came from the English nursery rhyme, 'It's Raining It's Pouring' – author unknown.

It was all in support of a reoccurring theme. Joni was more than familiar with music business sham and hyperbole as far back as 'For the Roses', when the subject first overtly asserted itself.

I guess I seem ungrateful
With my teeth sunk in the hand
That brings me things
I really can't give up just yet
Now I sit up here the critic
And they introduce some band
But they seem so much confetti
Looking at them on my TV set

After 25 years, 'Taming the Tiger', transformed that general idea into;

As the radio blared so bland
Every disc a poker chip
Every song just a one night stand
Formula music, girly guile
Genuine junk food for juveniles
Up and down the dial
Mercenary style

In a seeming reconstitution of the 'The Reoccurring Dream' vocal commercial exclamations, we intermittently hear that track's two-note melody motif on the word 'Boring!', as if those catchphrases had outgrown their worth, realised their inherent falseness and cannibalised themselves in an epiphany of capitalist masochism. The point is that here was offered what I suggested as missing from the prior song; a way of delineating the aftermath. And it was done partially by turning a detail of another track on its head.

It all takes place on a smooth semi-acoustic calming liquid ride that undulates like a tiger stripe. Where the album's other key track, 'Harlem In Havana', seemed to sprout predominantly from inspiration and no-mind, 'Taming the Tiger' was more technique. They were each other's compliment, yin and yang, or if you will, orange and black.

'The Crazy Cries of Love' (Joni Mitchell, Don Freed)

Released as a CD single, 1998.

Saskatoon singer/songwriter, Don Freed, was a friend of Joni's mother Myrtle. Freed wrote these lyrics mostly and Joni set them to music, tweaking some lines to fit the structure. Originally known as 'Love's Cries', it was recorded back before *Turbulent Indigo* came out, though presumably drummer Brian Blade's performance was added later. It wasn't unusual for acoustic guitar and vocal to be recorded *before* bass and drums.

The self-explanatory lyric covered extracurricular teenage activities beneath Saskatoon's old railroad bridge on a stormy night, adding to other Saskatoon bridge songs like 'Cherokee Louise' and 'Face Lift'. Joni and Larry performed 'The Crazy Cries of Love' live on L.A. radio station KCRW's *Morning Becomes Eclectic* program the day the album was released.

'Stay in Touch' (Joni Mitchell)

In 1998, Joni described the soft acoustic ballad 'Stay In Touch' as being about the beginning instability in a passionate new relationship, specifically that with her daughter Kilauren Gibb. The two had recently been reunited, but the lyric was not emphatic. The following year, Joni told *Mojo* magazine, 'Any time I have a passionate new relationship, that song will come to life in a new way. If it's overly explained, you rob the people whose lives it brushes up against of their own interpretation and their own experience.'.

'Face Lift' (Joni Mitchell)

Further to the above entry, interpreting 'Face Lift' was impossible unless you ignored the specifics. The lyric outlining Myrtle Anderson's disapproval of Joni and Don Freed 'gleaming' down the street at Christmas, was as personal as anything on *Blue.* No attempt was made to disguise the situation in order for a listener to make their own interpretation. Joni never took to the term 'confessional' – it implied some kind of criminal act. If she sang candidly of her life, it was a valid choice. Why describe it as confessional? 'Real' would be a better word, and there's no denying the reality present in this song. It was recorded back before the release of *Turbulent Indigo*, perhaps Joni slept on it for a while to ponder whether to let out such personal information. But critics and listeners would attribute their own idea of the truth to the songs anyway, so if she wanted the truth known, she might as well hand it to them on a platter.

The original title, 'Happiness is the Best Facelift', appeared randomly in conversation one day. Don Freed recommended writing it down for a possible song. Lucky it was kept, or we wouldn't have these particular whirling and effortless soprano sax lines from Wayne Shorter. There was clearly no limit to his ability to find an individual solo approach to suit a particular song.

'My Best To You' (Isham Jones, Gene Willadsen)

People would occasionally approach Joni in places like the supermarket and ask when her next record was coming out. Sometimes she'd say, 'I don't know. I'm blocked. What should I write about?'. Some would answer, 'Give us hope'. She would then reply, 'Why would I be giving you *hope*? They kill people in this culture that give hope, or hadn't you noticed?'.

The 1949 country hit by Sons of the Pioneers made its presence felt after Joni picked up their greatest hits CD from the supermarket. The song struck her and gave *her* hope, so recording it was the obvious thing to do. Her approach was simple and interesting – predominantly synthesizer, sampled bass and percussion, with Greg Leisz' pedal steel retaining a touch of the country spirit. As Joni told Chris Douridas on L.A.'s *KCRW* in 1998; 'I couldn't write it, so I borrowed it.'.

'Tiger Bones' (Joni Mitchell)

The closing instrumental is the complete and naked acoustic guitar track from 'Taming the Tiger'.

Both Sides Now (2000)

Personnel:
Vocals: Joni Mitchell
Bass: Chuck Berghofer, Mike Brittain, Mary Scully
Double bass: Chris Laurence
Drums: Peter Erskine
Piano: Dave Arch, Herbie Hancock
Soprano and tenor saxophone: Wayne Shorter
Trumpet: Mark Isham
Recorded in 1999 at Air Studios, Hampstead, London, UK; Ocean Way, Los Angeles, CA.
Producers: Joni Mitchell, Larry Klein
Engineers: Geoff Foster, Ben Georgiades, Allen Sides
Orchestral arranger: Vince Mendoza and Gordon Jenkins
Label: Reprise
US Release date: 8 February 2000. UK Release date: March 2000.
Chart placings: US: 66, UK: 50, CAN: 19, NO: 20.

Head of a Woman, Shape of a Lioness

Featuring the forces of a 71-piece orchestra and 22-piece big band, *Both Sides Now* did more than merely crank out a selection of standards – something that was becoming a trend after recent orchestral albums by Bryan Ferry and George Michael. Joni and Larry Klein devised the concept of a programmatic album that followed the arc of a relationship from inception through to break up, resolution and returning friendship – in fact, the arc of their very relationship. In so doing they jokingly came to refer to the songs as 'the stations of the cross'.

They enlisted American composer and orchestral arranger, Vince Mendoza. Only the arrangement for 'Stormy Weather' came from outside, which was largely Gordon Jenkins' score as heard on Frank Sinatra's 1959 Capitol album *No One Cares*. Mendoza made only minimal changes, to accommodate the new key a fourth higher to suit Joni's vocal range.

Additional soloists were saxophonist Wayne Shorter, pianist Herbie Hancock, and trumpeter Mark Isham. Joni's vocals were controlled, with a slight jazz vibrato, that at times recalled Billie Holiday. Years of smoking had reduced her vocal cords to a lower fundamental frequency, a timbre she was happy with and one more than fit for the delivery of these noir torch valentines.

An intimate and resigned self-portrait graced the cover, and the album was dedicated to Joni's daughter Kilauren. The *Both Sides Now* American tour was undertaken from 12 May to 6 June 2000, with a different orchestra in every city. At the 43rd Annual Grammy Awards on 21 February 2001, the album won Best Traditional Pop Vocal Album. Additionally, 'Both Sides, Now' won the Grammy for Best Instrumental Arrangement Accompanying Vocalist(s).

With *Both Sides Now* being largely a covers album, I've included entries for only the two original songs.

'A Case of You' (Joni Mitchell)

After almost a minute of introductory strings variation, the woodwinds faithfully follow the original *Blue* dulcimer chord moves, a fourth lower in key. The song fits at the point in the album's programmatic arc at which doubt creeps into the relationship. Minus the youthful vigour retained in spite of the situation in the original, the new version communicates as more resigned. The old angst originally manifested through drawing a map of Canada on a coaster is absent here, due to this performance coming as more of a total recall than as happening in the here and now. The verse starting with 'I am a lonely painter' works for the present perfectly, as does the below stanza. It referred to Joni's lyric lines in general, but with the passing of time, it now seemed to refer to these specific lines themselves.

> 'Cause part of you pours out of me
> In these lines from time to time
> Oh, you're in my blood like holy wine
> You taste so bitter and so sweet

Wayne Shorter's soprano sax depicts the wine as if quickly tipped to a savoured swallow, twice. Arriving at the end – where the original recording mysteriously landed on the chord two keys down from the home key – we land on the subdominant a fourth above the new home key as if to say the distance has provided insight but not *full* understanding. But wait! This final chord is in fact the home key of the original version. Some dissonance exists within the chord, but in effect, after 29 years, the cycle is resolved, at last.

'Both Sides, Now' (Joni Mitchell)

Released as a single, 2000.

Functioning within the album arc as a wistful full stop, this take – a major third lower in key than the original – could also be perceived as a retrospective shoulder glance. The lyric certainly held up as the possible viewpoint of a 56-year-old, which made its insights penned by the 23-year-old Joni all the more astonishing. The lyric's maturity transcended its composer's youth from the beginning.

Joni performed the song with orchestra at an all-star tribute held in her honour at New York's Hammerstein Ballroom on 6 April 2000. The fine muted-trumpet of Mark Isham was a tasteful modification to the coda, but Wayne Shorter's closing soprano remarks on the album version were a conclusion nothing short of passionate restrained eloquence.

Travelogue (2002)

Personnel:
Vocals: Joni Mitchell
Bass: Larry Klein
Double bass: Chuck Berghofer
Drums: Brian Blade
Flugelhorn: Kenny Wheeler
Hammond B-3 Organ: Billy Preston
Percussion: Paulinho da Costa
Piano: Herbie Hancock
Soprano saxophone: Wayne Shorter
Tenor saxophone: Plas Johnson
Recorded in 2002 at Air Studios, Lyndhurst Hall, London, UK; Ocean Way, Hollywood, CA; Record One, Sherman Oaks, CA; Market Street, Venice, CA.
Producers: Joni Mitchell, Larry Klein
Engineers: Jeff Burns, Geoff Foster, Helik Hadar, Jake Jackson, Andy Strange, Tom Sweeney, Darrell Thorp
Arranger: Vince Mendoza
Label: Nonesuch
US Release date: 19 November 2002. UK Release date: November 2002

The recording of *Travelogue* took place at George Martin's Air Studios Lyndhurst, London, with a film crew in tow. The orchestral arrangements were again undertaken by Vince Mendoza – 'Woodstock' eventually winning the 2004 Grammy award for Best Instrumental Arrangement Accompanying Vocalists(s). Despite the album's classification as jazz, the material was divided between a jazz and classical approach, occasionally simultaneous. Many song keys were lowered to accommodate Joni's newfound contralto vocal range, but with the overall new musical character being such a contrast, the key-changes were less dulling than can sometimes be the case in these situations. On the contrary – the lower pitch provided a depth matching the lyrics, certainly in the case of 'The Circle Game' which was here revealed to be every bit the profound philosophy its singsong surface had always obscured. Nevertheless, Joni admitted to having problems approaching the darker songs vocally, simply from having been in a great mood for an extended period. Though I'm sure the event of a fire at Air Lyndhurst that almost destroyed the album's master tapes must've helped lower the mood somewhat, though would've been tinged with a definite relief.

For years Joni had the album title *Songs of the Sunday Painter*. That possibility had been in the hat for the last four or five projects. But arranging older material for orchestra and reinterpreting it all vocally was a big ask, and distilling the essence of the project down to a singular title phrase proved difficult. She described the recording process as analogous to unloading the car on holiday. Thus the title *Travelogue* was appropriate, and a last-minute decision. She later said that if the title *Hejira* had not been taken, it would've worked for this.

On completion – adorned with another self-portrait cover – *Travelogue* fulfilled the Reprise recording contract, but the release was passed sideways to Warner Group's Nonesuch Records. For a time, Joni considered whether it would be her last record. The accolades were still appearing, but seemingly in the manner of a career winding itself down. In 2002 she was appointed a Companion of the Order of Canada and was also bestowed a Grammy Lifetime Achievement Award.

Songwriting had been on the back burner for a few years now. Feeling few people were still interested, Joni occupied herself more with painting. After the events of 11 September 2001, three were painted within weeks. She saw images in the World Trade Center smoke and took many photographs of the TV screen, trying to capture it all. She referred to the event as 'the war', telling interviewers that it had revived her songwriting. But she felt a pull away from the business in general and figured a complete exit from it might further awaken the music. She did *not* want another record deal, but also saw her work as yet not fully-developed and came to question how she could really quit. But there would have to be a real shift for her to continue in a business she now viewed as over-calculated.

'Otis and Marlena' (Joni Mitchell)

Placing 'Otis and Marlena' first up seemed perhaps demanding on a new listener, but for the converted it was a cinch. The arrangement was uncomplicated. That's not to say there wasn't a definite gear-change involved even for those already familiar with this repertoire. If you approved of the orchestral concept in the first place, there was still a small period of adjustment to warm you into it. But once you accepted the overall change, you could get dirty in the details.

Right out of the gate, the first obvious difference was the key change – down a minor third. But the vocal lost no conviction because of it. The narrative, about a couple holidaying in Miami while blissfully ignorant to world affairs, placed the story firmly in 1977 (consult the song's *Don Juan's Reckless Daughter* entry), despite the arrangement's pleasing between-the-wars aspect. The military snare drum at the line 'While Muslims stick up Washington' tied it all together.

The style change overall was potentially polarising in a polarising career, for sure. But mostly, this fascinating update left you slightly incredulous but eager to continue. Who could refuse that fabulous three-note strings chord at 3m:20s, swooping up on the left on the line 'It's all a dream she has awake'? Not me.

'Amelia' (Joni Mitchell)

If you were having doubts at this point, 'Amelia' was the track to evaporate them. Placing it second was an astute move. What true convert could resist the song however it was presented? Maybe 'Hejira' was more exalted in the canon, but we didn't want to get that out of the way *too* quickly, *right?* The tension of the wait, and the wondering what on earth they'd do with *that* landmark, was half the fun. So, concentrate! 'Amelia', okay. (Breathes).

The dreamlike landscape has harp standing in for acoustic guitar. Therefore, a minor lyric adjustment changes 'It was the hexagram of the heavens, it was the strings of my guitar' to 'Like the hexagram of the heavens, like the strings of my guitar'. Vistas open up increasingly on the completion of each sung verse. One appropriately opens right out as if breaking through the cloud mass, underneath the final verse's line, 'I dreamed of 747s over geometric farms'.

Rather than the arrangement predictably depicting the Greek myth on the line 'Like Icarus ascending on beautiful foolish arms', the possible cliché is turned on its head with a tumbling horn arpeggio several seconds before the fact (at 3m:57s), preceding even the ascension, which lands on a peak but for a four-note descending oboe motif. It's heady stuff, and certainly fitting that this lyric provided the album title.

'You Dream Flat Tires' (Joni Mitchell)

From the start, the original polyphonic chord lick – infamous among Joni's musician fans – is broken up between the instruments in a snaky swing-jazz amble through an almost Stan Kenton modernist landscape. Organist, Billy Preston, adds some real Hammond B3 chunk-and-twirl throughout. On top, the appropriately cool vocal suggests sunglasses might be a required accessory. That is until you twig that Joni is virtually channelling jazz singer, Sarah Vaughan – especially on the final verse line, 'What are you going to let love be?' – when you realise the performance actually transcends cool. That line was updated from the original 'When are you going to let love be?', and also replaced the original closing line, 'What are you going to let love do?'

'Love' (Joni Mitchell)

The first minute and twelve seconds is devoted to an almost hymnal musical setup, totally befitting the lyric's basis of the New Testament's *Corinthians I:13*. A lone trumpet sounds over a slow-moving bed of strings and harp, Wayne Shorter's singular and perfectly-intonated soprano sax 'A'-note interrupting at the halfway point. A descending chord pass then leads to that opening vocal line. No less striking here than it ever was, its emotion is curbed in a mid-line tension on 'I'm just sounding brass' as if regretful of the fact. Shorter's ascending line at 2m:03s sounds virtually indistinguishable from a human voice, a reminder that the goal of all monophonic instruments is to speak, Shorter being one of few who actually achieves it.

Atop a smoky bed of brushes and double bass, the strings carry the vocal, unhindered enough to more clearly reveal each verse's seeming snatch of Phoebe Snow's 'Poetry Man' melody – a certainly respectable, but unlikely overt, reference. I'm unable to hear the four-note motif any other way.

'Woodstock' (Joni Mitchell)

In the widest key-change drop yet – a full augmented-fourth lower – the famous song is manifested in a slow saunter, the likes of which millions of visitors approaching Yasgur's Farm in 1969 were forced to adopt due to their sheer number. The feel is that of a quest, and you can feel Joni there walking with her companion more than was evident from her original recording. She was of course *not* at Woodstock, the often-expounded-upon irony being that she wrote what afterwards became a virtual theme song after the event, removed from it.

The pattern in these arrangements seemed to be that whenever a picturesque lyric couplet appeared – such as at 'I dreamed I saw the bombers riding shotgun in the sky, and they were turning into butterflies' – the arrangement response was left respectfully restrained. In this case, a hole of sorts presents itself at that point, the listener's imagination left to furnish it with the image. Bravo. In a song that's an extension of a real-world political statement – one that was pro-free-love, anti-war, even anti-thought-police – arranger Vince Mendoza here dictates our thinking. If anyone was to do it, it would best be somebody like him.

'Slouching Towards Bethlehem' (Joni Mitchell – Lyric adapted from 'The Second Coming' by W.B. Yeats)

Night Ride Home's *tour de force* was here given its rightful treatment. Like the offspring most likely to succeed, it had seemed slightly over-sized for that album. It *was* tamed well within those bounds but always had the potential to grow up frightening. This arrangement takes full advantage of that potential, Joni, in turn, approaching the vocal with perhaps a touch too much levity, certainly on the chorus, though understandable if the goal was to avoid tipping the scales.

The lyric based on Yeats' 1919 poem *The Second Coming* with its *Book of Revelation* imagery and post-World-War-One aftermath, was always ripe for theatrical extrapolation, and arranger Vince Mendoza left few stones unturned in creating *Travelogue*'s most programmatic presentation.

As with the 'Woodstock' arrangement, there's the feeling of moving towards something – or more accurately, something coming towards us – but on a grander scale with much more at stake. The battery of warlike drums of the *Night Ride Home* version remain, even more emphatic now – their sudden arrival at the one-minute mark with winds and horns in tow, striking indeed. In fact, with the low strings occupied maintaining a static underlying current of melancholy uncertainty, the horns are responsible for much of the darkness throughout. They provide the dissonant stateliness accompanying the key phrase, 'Shaped like a lion, It has the head of a man', and punctuate the footsteps as 'It's moving its slow thighs across the desert sands'. The winds too contribute to the tension, their syncopated and elongated dissonant chord clusters ushering in every chorus, where in turn the piano joins them in cacophonous staccato tumbles. A pair of high French horns then repeatedly cry their desperate warning, though are temporarily repressed by the final chorus which only allows them one final warning cycle before the accompanying monosyllabic monk-like vocal chants get the final say.

To conclude, the dramatic and goosebump-inducing ending functions like the revelation of a work of fiction's second major dramatic plot point – which as far as the album was concerned, this track probably was.

'Judgement of the Moon and Stars (Ludwig's Tune)' (Joni Mitchell)

Commencing with the character of a lively opera overture, this arrangement transports a listener through the European courts and bedrooms of the early 19th century into Beethoven's rooms themselves. It's there that, 'Revoked but not yet cancelled, The gift goes on'.

By the time of *For the Roses*, which housed this song's original version, Joni had, of course, experienced a definite level of success. But with some of the rock press becoming more interested in spreading vacuous Joni gossip, it's easy to understand her alignment with the great composer and the ostracising he endured.

> You've got to spread your light like blazes
> All across the sky
> They're going to aim the hoses on you
> Show 'em you won't expire
> Not till you burn up every passion
> Not even when you die

As if she knew how bad things might become (she did live in the future after all), she here demonstrated after-the-fact advice as an allegory for self-therapy. Thirty years after *For the Roses*, she was now a multi-award-winning respected recording artist in the throes of a welcomed self-retrospective. Clearly, the therapy had worked.

'The Sire of Sorrow (Job's Sad Song)' (Joni Mitchell)

The song itself gets the attention here, the arrangement understated and not too far removed from the *Turbulent Indigo* version. Based on the Old Testament's *Book of Job*, the lyrics carry it, with little spinning-off into instrumental portrayal detail, with the exception of the dissonant one-chord fanfare at 1m:41s – its underlying subtext suggesting the line 'Kings heard my words' to be a dubious honour.

The role of the antagonists, here played by a male chorus, is given the depth it lacked on *Turbulent Indigo*, supplying a truly ecclesiastic tone to an exceptional and important piece more than worthy of reverence amongst its repertoire peers.

'For the Roses' (Joni Mitchell)

A project like this would surely give an arranger an instance to throw off all caution and take a no-holds-barred approach. This was certainly one. Now twice the length – though it was taken much slower and a coda added – this was so far the song whose character was changed the most. The dropping of the key a minor third lower was just the beginning. From the introduction's wafting discords onward, the lyric concept of the music business' dark sides was rendered in an almost gleeful black humour. It's what was *not* being said that was the point. No opportunity for reproachful subtext in the form of slowly creeping, or suddenly startling, string figure tension was left untaken. The adoption of an orchestra effectively changed the song's original analogy of a music career simulating a racehorse charging to the finish line only to be shot, to more resemble a journey through a dark forest.

Wayne Shorter's improvised sax lines weave in and around above it all as if promising a way out. But it's a long haul. The shimmering violins around the 5m:10s mark independently pitch-vary, hovering back and forth in the manner of a horrific Ligeti glissando but significantly less accentuated. The closing line, 'And the moon swept down black water like an empty spotlight', comes to vivid cinematic life. The scene continues for a further 90 seconds, sax lines developing over an increasingly widening and even illogical Cinemascope that's progressively 1940s noir, 1980s slasher, and timeless science fiction. But it's all done with taste stopping short of true cliché, except for mine; hard act to follow.

'Trouble Child' (Joni Mitchell)

The first of only two songs representing *Court and Spark* in this collection made little attempt to compete with the four preceding grand statements. If anything, it was understated. The dropping of the key a fourth lower – probably a smidgen too much – certainly lowered the potential impact. But one identifying Mendoza arrangement twist came in the closing chorus triads swelling amongst the instruments, beyond the key mode, indeed 'Breaking like the waves at Malibu'.

'God Must Be a Boogie Man' (Joni Mitchell)

The only *Mingus* song included here has a swing-jazz basis. The presence of smooth string section swells, dissonant winds and punctuating horn accents brings the orchestra into collision with jazz once again. On top, the vocal has moments of pure conversational tone, making the delivery more intimate than the original. Central to it all is Wayne Shorter's completely applicable sax solo of almost a minute. His whirlwind arpeggios break out to their most aggressive extent yet in this collection.

'Be Cool' (Joni Mitchell)

Mellow and unflappable, the introduction leads by example. The saxophone a tenor this time, the bulk of the track is cool swing – as the lyric says,

'Fifty-fifty fire and ice'. Herbie Hancock's stunning high piano cross-rhythm demisemiquavers commencing at 4m:06s are a closing section focal point. Likewise, when the rhythm section ends, it makes way for an almost Philip-Glass-like 12/8 horn and strings murmur, fifty-fifty swung and straight. This second iteration of the song provides further tuition in the personal skill. After all, to stay cool is one thing, but to *be* cool is another.

'Just Like This Train' (Joni Mitchell)

It's not until you hear this version that you realise just how tense the original *Court and Spark* vocal actually was. It wasn't that noticeable probably because the song then came across as conventional compared to most of its companions. The current take brings a sensible and conversational rendering of the advice as if with the benefit of hindsight the sour grapes have shrivelled up. The steady snare drum rimshot evokes the train rhythm, and the first verse brass section toots the horn. This is a happy song now; all tension left to the past.

'Sex Kills' (Joni Mitchell)

Thankfully there was just enough tension in this arrangement to back up the lyric's point and create interest. Otherwise, the entire thing might've been in danger of being merely a pop song with orchestra. And as brilliant as Wayne Shorter's playing always is, by this point in the album the ingredient starts to feel like it's being heard too frequently – or maybe it's just redundant in this case. But then, the Baroque painter, Rembrandt, chose to use the colour gold in many works, so who are we to argue with artistic choice?

'Refuge of the Roads' (Joni Mitchell)

Starting from a stationary lone harp, this orchestration travelled the vast expanse covered in the lyric. Verse one was edited slightly, the heat taken off John Guerin, the 'Friend of spirit' who 'Drank and womanised'. He was now 'A friend of spirit, a drunk with sage's eyes'. The verse's closing line, 'I left him then for the refuge of the roads', became 'And he sent me then to the refuge of the roads'. As we know, it was all deeply personal, and the line, 'I well up with affection thinking back down the roads to then', must surely have taken on a greater profundity in the singing after 26 years.

After such a passing of time, this lyric seemed to be even more of a lesson in humanity and self-care. But like a seer, Joni stopped short of spelling things out. At this writing, a further eighteen years have passed. Many people must surely hear this lyric and miss the point completely. In fact, I know one or two who after all this time praise it, but still fail to glean its wisdom, let alone put it into practice.

> Oh radiant happiness
> It was all so light and easy

Till I started analysing
And I brought on my old ways

Throughout Joni's career, many looked (and still look) to her lyrics for guidance. Much wisdom was to be found in them, but 'Refuge of the Roads' offered perhaps the most valuable advice of all for those open to uncovering it. The true sage of the song was not Guerin, but Joni herself.

'Hejira' (Joni Mitchell)

After a minute of orchestral setup, it became apparent that the track was being taken too fast. The vocal approach too was lighter, even flippant at times, the decades clearly having diminished the emotional urgency. As a result, the entire track seemed stripped of the intensity that inhabited the very marrow of the original.

But care was taken in changing some lyric detail, to tighten up meaning. 'Bolts of lace waltzing on a ballroom girl' became 'Waltzing on a bridal girl'. 'The hope and the hopelessness I've witnessed thirty years' was logically altered to 'All these years'. 'Always' was dropped from 'How can I have that point of view when I'm (always) bound and tied to someone?'.

The strings between the first two verses followed the original fretless bass melodies. Portamento slides in an almost Indian strings style resulted in an appropriate and pleasing Eastern flavour. The verse two 'strains of Benny Goodman' were now chordal and in a more big-band arrangement, sitting in contrast to the solo clarinet of the original version.

A final stroke of genius came with the final vocal line, 'Until love sucks me back that way', delivered two measures late so 'back that way' landed directly on the key change playout – a variation so effective and obvious in hindsight that it seems surprising it wasn't realised in the original version.

From there, Larry Klein's slick and agile improvised bass wound the song down to a singular downward viola swoop end. The mature 'Hejira' had spoken. There always seemed so much riding on this song in whatever incarnation it was performed. It's just one of those tracks. Personally, I expected more from this version, but maybe I expected too much.

'Chinese Cafe/Unchained Melody' (Joni Mitchell/Alex North and Hy Zaret)

The key-change down a minor third here seemed to be too much of a drop. The original vocal never sounded high, but there was likely more involved in the decision than the vocal alone. This take does sound low, especially in the closing bars of the 'Unchained Melody' section. Not that the low notes weren't comfortably reached, they certainly were. In fact, it showed an area of Joni's range that was worthy of further exploration.

For her, the recording of this vocal was an issue. She couldn't quite find the character she was after. In delivering the lines, she tried to think of an actress to use as a role model but was at a loss. In the end, it was the technique of American actor Jimmy Stewart, that came to the rescue. It dawned on her that he was never melodramatic and always on his centre. To refer back to another *Wild Things Run Fast* song, he knew how to 'be cool'. The orchestration kept its cool here too – the lyric and 'Unchained Melody' and 'Will You Still Love Me Tomorrow?' flashback insertions, more than enough to maintain interest.

'Cherokee Louise' (Joni Mitchell)

The tragedy that befell Joni's childhood friend was here depicted within an almost Aaron-Copland-Americana climate, despite the story's location, of course, being Saskatoon – specifically the Broadway bridge. A slightly slower tempo added extra pathos. The line 'We've got *Archie* and *Silver Screen*' was changed to 'We've got comics and magazines', presumably to expedite meaning. Overall, a more dignified tribute would be difficult to imagine.

'The Dawntreader' (Joni Mitchell)

This exact arrangement would've worked beautifully on *Song to a Seagull*, had there been the wherewithal at that early career stage. The key was kept the same, the only significant lyric change being from the lofty 'I believe him when he tells of loving me' to 'I believe him when he says he loves me' – an edit that made perfect sense. The song's nautical theme was audibly palpable at 'Seabird I have seen you fly above the pilings', in a savvy portrayal via violin harmonics. The last verse's key line 'And a dream of a baby' was left under-enunciated, in contrast to the *Song to a Seagull* version which slightly overstated the point.

Surrounding 'The Dawntreader' with many of its more recent peers, demonstrated just how undeniably developed the songwriting was at this early stage. It was shrewd indeed of David Crosby to realise this and keep not just orchestra, but everything extraneous *off* the album that was this song's original home.

'The Last Time I Saw Richard' (Joni Mitchell)

The original *Blue* recording had been exceedingly high in vocal pitch, requiring a drop here eight keys lower, the biggest on *Travelogue*. This worked well to accentuate the lyric's conversation. The change from 'Go look at your eyes, they're full of moon' to 'They're two blue moons' was logical. As was the surprise waitress's line, 'Drink up now, it's gettin' on time to close', spoken believably in character.

'Borderline' (Joni Mitchell)

It felt like a congruous vocal approach had yet to be found for this. Some lines were thrown away, some overly-playful, others rhythmically rigid. The line 'Prickling with pretence' was altered to 'Prickling with defence', as if the 'pr' alliteration was now deemed a gimmick. But the song quality was still undeniable if only for the sandwiching of the melody note on 'line' at almost every title utterance, making the note indeed a border between the title's other two.

'The Circle Game' (Joni Mitchell)

The idea of a circle is here cleverly indicated by the chords as they revolve around the home root key. After its announcement as the very first chord, the root is avoided, occurring only at the midpoint of each progression – the end of each verse. This rule is broken at the end of chorus three which lands squarely on the home key but only for one beat before moving away. The root is heard once more at the normal end-verse juncture before the final chorus but is never returned to. The song continues on to land on the home key's relative minor.

This circulation conveniently helped to remove the original version's constant joyful feeling which effectively overdosed the song when taken in conjunction with the lyric's playful aspects. Now we were given an arrangement that reflected the truly serious concept – that we move ever onward and there's nothing we can do about it. It's pretty heavy stuff when you consider the lyric that way.

This discography includes many heavy emotional moments brought on by the journey of life, at times filtered through songwriting as a form of artistic therapy. But 'The Circle Game' stands as a personal expression that, rather than being a personal catharsis, was merely a gift, for Neil Young. It was perhaps the purest such gesture in this entire repertoire.

Shine (2007)

Personnel:
Vocals, Guitar, Piano, Keyboards: Joni Mitchell
Acoustic guitar: James Taylor
Alto and soprano saxophone: Bob Sheppard
Bass, Double bass: Larry Klein
Drums: Brian Blade
Pedal steel: Greg Leisz
Percussion: Paulinho da Costa
Recorded 2006-2007 at Castle Oaks Productions, Calabasas, California.
Producer: Joni Mitchell
Engineers: Josh Blanchard, Dan Marnien, Chris Marshall
Label: Hear Music
US Release date: 25 September 2007. UK Release date: September 2007.
Chart placings: US: 14, UK: 36, IE: 59. CA: 13, AU: 71. CH: 100. FR: 103. IT: 30. NL: 44. NO: 10. SE: 25.

In 2007, Joni revealed an additional catalyst for her 2002 retirement from the music business. Drained after a gruelling interview that year for VH1 – sitting on a stool answering questions for five hours – she took to her bed for three days. She didn't understand why she felt so bad. Then, watching TV, she came across an episode of *Larry King Live* featuring a Gulf War/Vietnam prisoner explaining the two regions' differing torture techniques. He explained how in Vietnam they'd put you on a chair and fire questions at you for hours until you'd tell them anything they wanted. This was the same treatment Joni had undergone, and that realisation basically made the decision to retire *for* her. She believed she'd never make another record. But then, 'Oops, here it came. I was trying to keep my legs crossed and it was like a late birth. They all come out that way. It's like they're writing me'.

But it wasn't like inertia had overtaken Joni in the five years since *Travelogue*. In 2004 she assembled the fine Geffen compilation, *The Beginning of Survival* – a collection of political and cultural material spanning the period from *Dog Eat Dog* to *Taming the Tiger*. By now her Warner catalogue had fallen into the hands of Rhino Records, but she rejected their suggestion of a *Best Of* compilation. Reprise's 1996 *Hits* collection already had that covered. (Not to mention its companion, *Misses* – a Joni-curated collection of her favourites from her output). Instead, she worked with Rhino on two compilations – *Dreamland*; featuring material from *Clouds* through to *Travelogue*, and *Songs of a Prairie Girl*; consisting of tracks referring to her home province of Saskatchewan and released to align with its May 2005 centennial.

On 10 November 2006, Los Angeles' Lev Moross Gallery opened a two-month installation of sixty new Joni Mitchell mixed-media artworks with an anti-war theme, under the title *Green Flag Song,* aka *Flag Dance*. The inspiration for the works came from her television screen suddenly running in pinks, greens and yellows for five minutes or so every hour. It was most striking when showing black and white movies. She photographed the screen for six months until there was a surfeit of images to choose from.

Jean Grand-Maître, artistic director of the Alberta Ballet Company, showed an interest in using the images as an accompaniment to a ballet partially based on Joni's life, with the working title *Dancing Joni*. But Joni felt that with the world still in a state of post-9/11 red alert, she had no interest in escapist entertainment. Instead, she offered to put together a ballet based on the theme of environmental neglect. This would become *The Fiddle and the Drum*. The premiere took place on 8 February 2007, performed by the Alberta Ballet at the Southern Alberta Jubilee Auditorium. It consisted of the album versions of the following songs; 'The Fiddle and the Drum', 'Sex Kills', 'Passion Play', 'The Three Great Stimulants', 'For the Roses' (*Travelogue*), 'Slouching Towards Bethlehem', 'The Beat of Black Wings', 'If I Had a Heart', 'If' and 'Big Yellow Taxi (2007)'. Images from the *Green Flag Song* installation were made into a video which was projected over the dancers' heads onto a circular screen.

Three of the ballets' songs, 'If I Had a Heart', 'If' and the encore 'Big Yellow Taxi (2007)', were from the new album, still seven months from release. The new songs started life as instrumentals. In commencing writing, the only existing lyrics Joni had were the 'Bad Dreams' opening lines, and the Rudyard Kipling poem 'If' that she had yet to adapt into a song. The writing began as piano-dominant. Deciding to handle the bulk of musical overdubs herself, she acquired a five-year-old Yamaha synthesizer for orchestrations. Once she settled on a sound palette, the material fell into place. She described the lyrics as covering topics such as, 'The war of the fairytales' and 'Possibly the end of our species'.

Despite the activity of recent years, Joni had become separated from music to an extent. As the album neared completion, she was listening to mixes on her bedside CD radio alarm clock. Jean Grand-Maître came to the rescue loaning her his home stereo. With the album complete, Starbucks' Hear music label also came to the party, signing Joni for the release of *Shine*, which would be Hear's second release after Paul McCartney's *Memory Almost Full*, issued three months prior.

Release day – 25 September 2007 – was significant. A film of the Alberta Ballet performing *The Fiddle and the Drum* was premiered at the Sunshine Cinema in New York with Joni in attendance. Also released that day was the Herbie Hancock album, *River: The Joni Letters*, featuring a selection of vocalists adorning Hancock's arrangements of select Joni compositions. She herself sang on Hancock's abstract jazz take of 'The Tea Leaf Prophecy', accompanied by drummer Vinnie Coliauta, Bassist Dave Holland, Guitarist Lionel Loueke and saxophonist Wayne Shorter. Uncredited at the time was Prince, who played guitar on 'Edith and the Kingpin', sung by Tina Turner. That album hit number one on the jazz chart and won Album of the Year at the 50th annual Grammy Awards on 10 February 2008.

Shine too was a worldwide success, peaking at number 14 on the Billboard 200 in the USA – Joni's highest album position there since *Hejira*. Starbuck's Hear Music label closed down in July 2008.

Post-*Shine*, Joni devoted herself to painting, like her contemporary, Don Van Vliet aka Captain Beefheart – another musician/poet/painter who took a similar route two decades before.

'One Week Last Summer' (Joni Mitchell)

This instrumental piece, the first composed for *Shine*, was originally titled 'Gratitude'. In her home north of Vancouver, Joni wrote at the piano for the first time in ten years. Not the baby grand that was the conduit for most of *For the Roses* and *Court and Spark* in the same space over 30 years before, but a smaller spinet frame housing a Wurlitzer five-stop electric. As the chords came forth, so did a brown bear that rummaged through the garbage cans.

Nothing particularly singled the piece out as a Joni recording if you didn't already know it was her. The chords were pleasing – it was an incidental piece with little in the way of a melody. Bob Sheppard played the alto saxophone, but the remaining instrumentation came from samples. You'd think *that* would've made the piece work hard to compete with the other nominees for Best Pop Instrumental Performance at the 2008 Grammys – some of them stiff competition including Ben Harper & the Innocent Criminals, and American jazz/fusion outfit, Spyro Gyra. But 'One Week Last Summer' won on the night. *Shine* itself was also a success in general. There was still little that Joni Mitchell could do wrong.

'This Place' (Joni Mitchell)

The first topic out of the gate was ecology – specifically, the prevention of catastrophe. Since creating a home in British Columbia decades prior, Joni had kept her presence there pretty quiet, knowing that a famous person moving into a rural area can easily kick off a gentrification movement. On the nearby Sunshine Coast, developers were now beginning to clear land. There was a company wanting to mine for minerals, which would've meant conveying gravel out to sea for pickup. Thankfully the deal fell through.

> They're gonna tear 'em down
> And sell them to California
>
> When this place looks like a moonscape
> Don't say I didn't warn ya

'This Place' was the album's second guitar-written song (behind 'If') and fifth written overall. The basis was acoustic guitar, with alto sax, and Greg Leisz' swooning pedal steel swells keeping it grounded. Such minimalism was exactly what many fans craved. The guitar shuffle rhythm echoed songs like 'Number

One' and 'Turbulent Indigo' – a characteristic playing style that Joni once referred to as sounding like Robert Johnson on Mars.

'If I Had a Heart' (Joni Mitchell)

Part of the *The Fiddle and the Drum* ballet stage set was a projection of seven photographs of the earth at night, taken from every angle. After seeing the North America photos, Joni took to turning the lights off at night. She was shocked by the electronic blight the west had become upon the earth. Ecology had been a cause for her since the '60s, and she now felt somewhat inoculated at a time when the rest of the world was finally waking up. The song was a beautiful lament. Raising awareness through music was a way she could do *something*. She told one interviewer, 'I may feel like a flea on a dinosaur, but I'm still kicking it in the shins'.

The semi bossa nova drum-unit-style rhythm was playful, balancing the lyric's dark truth – truth reflected in the floating chord dissonances, most notably the haunting augmented-11th under the line 'We've set our lovely sky, our lovely sky, on fire'.

'Hana' (Joni Mitchell)

The programmed rhythm here brought a more contemporary, almost '90s jungle sound to *Shine* while retaining aspects of the broken-down '80s-style instrumental part arrangement. Bob Sheppard's alto sax throughout kept the sound in familiar Joni territory. The lyric, which lifted the album mood, was the tale from a '30s movie of a young woman who adopted a struggling family after showing up at their house in a blizzard. 'Hana' was a breezy respite in an album that had further topical trouble ahead.

'Bad Dreams' (Joni Mitchell)

'Bad Dreams' sat with 'If I Had A Heart' in attitude – stylistic and otherwise. Whether the lyric was negative was a matter of interpretation. Joni felt it was better to face facts than bury your head in the sand. Rather than come across as autobiographical, she preferred that others might see themselves in the song. Lines like, 'You take with such entitlement, you give bad attitude', were her being accusing of herself as much as anyone else.

The opening two lines were all she had when commencing writing for the album. They came from the below haiku she'd written, the third line of which was not used in the song.

The cats are in the flowerbed
A red hawk rides the sky
A little dog is chewing on a book of matches

'But we have poisoned everything' stood in for the haiku's third line, and the list proceeded from there. 'Whales beach and die in sand', was a bittersweet reminder of the event from the days immediately following Charles Mingus' death. But the lyric's key phrase came from Joni's three-year-old grandson.

One evening when he was getting tired and acting up, his mother said, 'It's a wonder he doesn't give me bad dreams'. The child then answered, 'But mama, bad dreams are good in the great plan'. Joni stated this to be one of the few profound things anyone had ever told her.

The lyric pointed out the trouble occurring and that the human race were responsible for righting those wrongs.

So who will come to save the day?
Mighty Mouse? Superman?
Bad dreams are good in the great plan.

'Big Yellow Taxi (2007)' (Joni Mitchell)

The *The Fiddle and the Drum* choreographer, Jean Grande-Maitre, had requested a song that could be used as an encore. Joni chose 'Big Yellow Taxi', dressing it up to specifically resemble the sounds of a French circus. On the album, it was also a good mood-lifter coming after 'Bad Dreams' and continued the ecology theme. The only lyric changes made were 'Hot spot' becoming 'Night spot', and 'Charged all the people a dollar and a half' becoming 'Charged all the people an arm and a leg'. 'Big Yellow Taxi' had become one of the few pop songs ever requiring rewriting to accommodate inflation.

'Night of the Iguana' (Joni Mitchell)

Like 'Hana', 'Night of the Iguana' was based in literary fiction, this time the 1964 screen adaptation of Tennessee Williams' play of the short story about a priest cast-out from the church. In approaching the song minus this information, the lyric would be fairly difficult to comprehend.

Listening today, Joni's electric guitar could've used the benefit of more picturesque amplification, and the chorus harmony vocals appear to have a pitching issue. But they're minor quibbles. Otherwise, the track had a contemporary sound, the bass and percussion towards the end recalling the edgy atmospheres of the Mitchell Froom/Tchad Blake sonics of Suzanne Vega's 1992 album *99.9F.*

'Strong and Wrong' (Joni Mitchell)

More like an exercise than a song, 'Strong and Wrong' seemed to be in the form of either a finished poem or an unfinished first draft lyric. I offer the following stanza as an example.

Men love war
That's what history's for
History
A mass-murder mystery
His story

It's quite a statement, with a bias unusual for Joni. It is taken out of context here of course, and as we know, whether a lyric was her actual belief, or fictional, was often a gamble in the interpretation. The stanza's idea certainly is an attitude that exists in *some*one's viewpoint; therefore, it's up for grabs as lyric matter. She has said that this lyric concerned the worship of egos and that she considered keeping the song as an instrumental for use as a hidden track. Perhaps part of her was wary of the lyric's abstraction.

'Shine' (Joni Mitchell)

The lengthy title track contained the album's most potentially positive message, but the opportunity was squandered. An apparent level of sarcasm was an obstacle in interpreting the lyric. The listener could view it all as a positive statement if they chose. But if – as in 'The Sire of Sorrow' from *Turbulent Indigo* – God was being addressed here, Joni held nothing back and really let him have it, as if it was the last chance to get the message out.

Let your little light shine

Shine on rising oceans and evaporating seas
Shine on our Frankenstein technologies

Shine on good earth, good air, good water
And a safe place for kids to play
Shine on bombs exploding half a mile away

Over 100 lines were discarded in this song's long gestation period. Joni told an interviewer at the time that the song could've been fourteen minutes long instead of seven. After playing the demo at an after-party for her 2007 Canadian Songwriters Hall of Fame induction, James Taylor told her he just *had* to play on the song. The understated guitar fills were his first contribution since appearing on *Dog Eat Dog*. Joni has stated that the song reminds her of *Blue*.

'If' (Joni Mitchell – Lyric adapted from Rudyard Kipling's 'If'.)

The closing song – not only for *Shine* but for the entire discography, at least at this writing – ultimately sums up life's lessons. It's a parting piece of wisdom and important knowledge as a whole for anyone.

The backing was kept brisk and light (though in a minor key), the lyric an adaptation of British writer Rudyard Kipling's 1910 poem, 'If'. Some lines were slightly rewritten, but the main difference was in the ending. See below Kipling's original closing lines followed by Joni's rewrite.

If you can fill the unforgiving minute
With sixty seconds' worth of distance run

Yours is the Earth and everything that's in it
And – which is more – you'll be a Man, my son!

If you can fill the journey of a minute
With sixty seconds worth of wonder and delight
Then the Earth is yours and everything that's in it
But more than that I know you'll be alright

She added to that a coda; 'Cause you've got the fight, You've got the insight'. 'If' was an appropriate swansong indeed, made all the stronger by the decision to give the final word to one of the great poets. In doing so, Joni demonstrated two of her own included lines – 'Don't need to look so good, Don't need to talk too wise'.

Epilogue: Fractions of Faith and Hope

The recording might have stopped, but more releases appeared. The *The Fiddle and the Drum* ballet soundtrack album saw daylight on 1 January 2008, adding 'Woodstock', 'The Reoccurring Dream' and 'Shine' to the tracklisting. 24 November 2014 saw the issue of the CD box set, *Love Has Many Faces: A Quartet, A Ballet, Waiting to be Danced.* Joni curated the four-act set from across the discography, creating a totally new piece of work in the process. The set won the Best Album Notes Grammy at the 58th annual awards on 15 February 2016.

After suffering a brain aneurysm in 2015, it was a year before Joni made any further public appearances. But accolades continued to arrive. The San Francisco SFJAZZ Center bestowed the Lifetime Achievement Award in 2015. In 2018, Saskatoon honoured her with plaques erected near the former Louis Riel Coffee House where she first performed, and another at River Landing. Further to that, a walkway along the riverfront was named Joni Mitchell Promenade. Most recently in 2020, she was the first woman to receive the Les Paul Award.

Awards were one thing, but in 2007 she told *Rolling Stone* magazine that one of the greatest compliments she ever received was from a blind black pianist who said her music was raceless and genderless. It was moments like that with the personal touch that meant the most. But of course for Joni to return to music would mean the most to fans. If James Taylor's recent interview comment that she was interested in music again holds any water, there's always hope that the discography is as yet incomplete.

In 'Both Sides, Now', Joni famously stated she really didn't know love at all. But she knew how to fall into it, and – at least in the early period – made many artistic attempts that dealt with climbing out of it. Decades later, she claimed that with the 1982 *Wild Things Run Fast* song, 'Love', she'd realised all she ever tried to say in a song.

> It summarised everything: how you have faith and hope and love as a child and lose them very early. You spend your whole life with just fragments of them left. That's what my writing has always been about.

But climbing in or out of whatever situation inspired her at any given time, there was always the potential positive of someone else hearing a song and being changed by it. There are those that sought and found wisdom in – and courage from – her work, and there were others who wished to emulate it. However the music was forged and however it was received, the result is this challenging catalogue. Perhaps its shadow cast over the shoulder of virtually any songwriter today who cares to notice will result in an advancement in – or at least a resurrection of – the craft. We could surely use either. After all, such an exploration was always the goal in Joni Mitchell's work. She did it for the music. Anyone else similarly interested only has to listen to hers and take up the torch from there.

On Track series

Queen – Andrew Wild 978-1-78952-003-3
Emerson Lake and Palmer – Mike Goode 978-1-78952-000-2
Deep Purple and Rainbow 1968-79 – Steve Pilkington 978-1-78952-002-6
Yes – Stephen Lambe 978-1-78952-001-9
Blue Oyster Cult – Jacob Holm-Lupo 978-1-78952-007-1
The Beatles – Andrew Wild 978-1-78952-009-5
Roy Wood and the Move – James R Turner 978-1-78952-008-8
Genesis – Stuart MacFarlane 978-1-78952-005-7
JethroTull – Jordan Blum 978-1-78952-016-3
The Rolling Stones 1963-80 – Steve Pilkington 978-1-78952-017-0
Judas Priest – John Tucker 978-1-78952-018-7
Toto – Jacob Holm-Lupo 978-1-78952-019-4
Van Der Graaf Generator – Dan Coffey 978-1-78952-031-6
Frank Zappa 1966 to 1979 – Eric Benac 978-1-78952-033-0
Elton John in the 1970s – Peter Kearns 978-1-78952-034-7
The Moody Blues – Geoffrey Feakes 978-1-78952-042-2
The Beatles Solo 1969-1980 – Andrew Wild 978-1-78952-030-9
Steely Dan – Jez Rowden 978-1-78952-043-9
Hawkwind – Duncan Harris 978-1-78952-052-1
Fairport Convention – Kevan Furbank 978-1-78952-051-4
Iron Maiden – Steve Pilkington 978-1-78952-061-3
Dream Theater – Jordan Blum 978-1-78952-050-7
10CC – Peter Kearns 978-1-78952-054-5
Gentle Giant – Gary Steel 978-1-78952-058-3
Kansas – Kevin Cummings 978-1-78952-057-6
Mike Oldfield – Ryan Yard 978-1-78952-060-6
The Who – Geoffrey Feakes 978-1-78952-076-7

On Screen series

Carry On... – Stephen Lambe 978-1-78952-004-0
Powell and Pressburger – Sam Proctor 978-1-78952-013-2
Seinfeld Seasons 1 to 5 – Stephen Lambe 978-1-78952-012-5
Francis Ford Coppola – Cam Cobb and Stephen Lambe 978-1-78952-022-4
Monty Python – Steve Pilkington 978-1-78952-047-7
Doctor Who: The David Tennant Years – Jamie Hailstone 978-1-78952-066-8
James Bond – Andrew Wild 978-1-78952-010-1

Other Books

Not As Good As The Book – Andy Tillison 978-1-78952-021-7
The Voice. Frank Sinatra in the 1940s – Stephen Lambe 978-1-78952-032-3
Maximum Darkness – Deke Leonard 978-1-78952-048-4
The Twang Dynasty – Deke Leonard 978-1-78952-049-1
Maybe I Should've Stayed In Bed – Deke Leonard 978-1-78952-053-8
Tommy Bolin: In and Out of Deep Purple – Laura Shenton 978-1-78952-070-5
Jon Anderson and the Warriors - the road to Yes – David Watkinson 978-1-78952-059-0

and many more to come!